I0041020

Small is the New Big:

How small companies can beat the giants

Author: Dr. Michael Teng

Published in 2012 by

Corporate Turnaround Centre Pte Ltd.

Printed in Singapore

By Markono Print Media

Copyright © 2012 by Corporate Turnaround Centre Pte Ltd. All rights reserved. This publication is protected by Copyright and permission should be obtained from the publisher prior to any prohibited reproduction, storage in a retrieval system, or transmission in any form or by any means, electronic, mechanical, photocopying, recording, or likewise. For information regarding permission(s), write to: admin@corporateturnaroundcentre.com

TABLE OF CONTENTS

Dr. Teng is widely recognized by the news media as a turnaround CEO in Asia. His subject of interest is corporate turnaround and transformation, as well as internet marketing. He has also been interviewed by the international media on many occasions, such as by: Malaysian Business Radio, BFM 89-9, News Radio FM 93.8, Malaysian Business Radio, Edge Radio (USA), the Channel News Asia, The Boss Magazine, Economic Bulletin, the Today, World Executive Digest, Lianhe ZaoPao, StarBiz, and the Straits Times. His online seminars are broadcast in 120 countries via Success University and Skyquest.Com.

Dr. Mike Teng is the author of a best-selling book Corporate Turnaround: Nursing a Sick Company Back to Health published in 2002. The book was translated into Bahasa, Indonesia and Mandarin and was endorsed by both management guru Professor Philip Kotler and business tycoons Mr. Oei Hong Leong and Dr. YY Wong. Dr. Teng has subsequently authored more than twenty five management books.

Dr. Teng is currently the Managing Director of Corporate Turnaround Centre Pte Ltd (www.corporateturnaroundcentre.com), which provides corporate training and management advisory services in Singapore, Malaysia, Vietnam, Ghana, etc. He was appointed by the Singapore government as the national trainer to coach and instruct displaced senior managers and deploy them to run SMEs.

He has more than 29 years of experience in setting up new plants, engaging in strategic planning, and handling operational management responsibilities in the Asia Pacific region. In these areas of expertise, he has held positions such as Chief Executive Officer for 19 years in multi-national and publicly listed companies. He was the CEO of a U.S. MNC based in Singapore for ten years. He spearheaded the turnaround of several troubled companies. He also advised several boards of directors of publicly listed companies.

Dr Teng is the Chairman of Chartered Management Institute, Singapore, President of the National University of Singapore MBA Alumni and the President of University of South Australia Alumni, Singpore. Dr. Teng served as an Executive Council member for fourteen years and the last four years as the President of the Marketing Institute of Singapore (2000 – 2004), the national marketing association. He was a member of the advisory board of the Business School, National University of Singapore and School of Business, Singapore Polytechnic as well as the Doctoral Program, University of South Australia.

He has a Doctor of Business Administration (DBA) degree from the University of South Australia, and a Master of Business Administration (MBA), and Bachelor of Mechanical Engineering (BENG) from the National University of Singapore. He is also a Professional Engineer (P Eng, Singapore), Chartered Engineer (C Eng, UK), and Fellow Member of several prestigious professional institutes, namely the Chartered Institute of Marketing (FCIM), Chartered Management Institute (FCMI), Institute of Mechanical Engineers (FIMechE), Marketing Institute of Singapore (FMIS), and Institute of Electrical Engineers (FIEE); he is a Senior Member of Singapore Computer Society (SMSCS). He is also a Practicing Management Consultant (PMC) certified by the Singapore government.

Chapter 1 – EXECUTIVE SUMMARY

How Can a Small Business Compete with Global Corporations?

Global corporations intimidate their competitors with huge advertising budgets, extensive R&D facilities, and a library of patents and law firms in every major market. How can a small business possibly compete with an army devoted to sales and marketing?

Yet small businesses do thrive, even in our hyper-competitive global marketplace. A few even grow to become global behemoths in their own right; the majority of successes simply remain local but they are profitable.

Too many entrepreneurs and small businesses lack even modest success, however. How can a struggling small business cope? Sun Tze advised generals that they could ensure victory by knowing both themselves and their enemies.

This book explains the advantages and disadvantages of small businesses. More importantly, it reveals the essential strategies for success: creating a profitable niche, applying business transformation techniques, and balancing innovation with productivity.

This book sometimes refers to the Biblical story of David and Goliath. David had been a harpist in the court of Saul, King of the Israelites. But David returned to tending sheep for his father, Jesse. While on an errand for his brothers in the army, David responded to the challenge from Goliath, the "giant" and champion of the Philistine army[1].

Many small businesses have succeeded, even against "giant" competitors. Some have even grown to become larger and more profitable than the former leaders in their industries.

Back to the Future

"Small" is becoming the new normal, but "small" has a long history that may be coming full circle.

---

[1] The main part of this Bible story is in I Samuel 17.

In prehistoric times, families and clans were hunters and gatherers. They did not require economies of scale; instead, small groups were, by necessity, self-sufficient. Subsistence agriculture followed and remained the norm in the less developed world. Some North Americans bemoan the loss of the family farm, in the wake of factory farming that owes more to the sprawling Southern cotton plantations than to the pioneer's "mule and plough on forty acres of land". However, the rise of family-operated, labour-intensive certified organic farming demonstrates that an intentionally small farm can turn a profit, if the product can command a premium.

In the field of computing, a number of very small businesses have found viable niches, and then were bought out for large sums. While this market may eventually be dominated by major corporations such as Microsoft with its "Office" suite, early start-ups did profit from "WordPerfect" or "VisiCalc". Buyouts have continued through 2012, and are likely in the foreseeable future; these make a few fortunate entrepreneurs extremely wealthy.

On a more realistic scale, skilled trades continue to provide a viable livelihood for plumbers, electricians and other contractors who run their own businesses. Professionals in service industries, from barbers and beauticians to doctors and lawyers can do very well within the bounds of their small practices.

Major Topics

The major topics are:

- Small is beautiful: the importance of small business in the global economy

- The seven mountains that a small business must surmount

- Advantages and disadvantages of small business

- An overview of three small business strategies

  o Strategy #1: discover and exploit the niche

  o Strategy #2: how a small business can use transformational processes

  o Strategy #3: blend innovation and efficiency

- Examples

- The mind-set for a small business

- How a small business owner should handle office politics

- Summary and conclusion

The Beauty of "Small"

Too often people fail to appreciate the beauty and strength of small things. This is especially true in business, where the largest companies garner the most headlines. This chapter explains why and how small business can be beautiful.

Seven Mountains that Small Business Must Surmount

Your small company may have several advantages over the giants in your market. Of course, you are probably already aware of your own disadvantages. Many of these mountains are addressed in later chapters or major sections of this book.

Small Business Advantages and Disadvantages

Your small company may have several advantages over the giants in your market. Of course, you are probably aware already of your own disadvantages. Learn how to leverage your position for success.

Introducing Three Strategies for Small Business

This chapter introduces three strategies:

- The "niche" strategy

- The three-part "Business Transformation" strategy for your small company

- The strategy to combine "Productivity with Innovation".

Each of these strategies has its own chapter.

The "Niche" Strategy

Even a large conglomerate should focus on its own market niche. A small business owner may have an entrepreneurial spirit, seeing opportunities at every turn. This chapter demonstrates that success requires concentrating one's efforts on a profitable niche.

The "Small Business Transformation" Strategy

Originally developed and proven to bring ailing companies back from the brink of bankruptcy, the "Corporate Transformation" strategy is simplified and streamlined to serve small businesses.

The "Productivity and Innovation" Strategy

Whether large or small, a business must combine innovation with productivity. If nothing changes, then the company is learning nothing. Seeking productivity without innovation may result in short-term profits, but eventually an innovator's new products will steal the customers. Continual innovation without the pursuit of productivity leads to unprofitably high "research and development" costs and, thus, bankruptcy.

A Few Examples

Two of the best examples of successful small business models are micro-financing and the growth of home-based businesses.

The Mind-set Required by a Small Business Owner

What is the mind-set that successful small business owners have and use?

Office Politics in a Small Business

As soon as two or more people are involved in an organization, office politics erupts. How should the small business owner deal proactively with these interpersonal relationships?

Summary: Your Small Business Strategy

This concluding chapter summarizes the book, putting the emphasis on what you should do to improve your small business.

Appendix: Review of the "Seven Mountains"

The review questions centre on the "Seven Mountains" chapter since it has many suggestions and concepts. They also touch on other aspects of this book, helping ensure you get as much out of the material as possible.

Onward to Success

That's enough of an introduction; it's time to learn why "small" can be beautiful in business.

Chapter 2 – SMALL IS BEAUTIFUL

"Make it big!" is the message at almost any seminar that promises to help you "grow your business".

Is this the only goal worth pursuing? Even if it is your ultimate goal, can your small company survive and thrive until it grows? If the only successful enterprise is the largest, how could it have begun small and survived to grow larger?

Success Starts Small...and Small can be a Success

The most famous success stories in business show that big companies started as smaller companies. Both Apple Computers and Microsoft famously began with young men operating tiny but innovative start-up companies.

A small business can be profitable and successful regardless of whether it grows larger. Some people are actually happier owning and operating a business that is the right size for their organizational skills, energy levels, and appetite for risk.

Giants have fallen. PanAm was a huge airline, but is no longer flying. Over a similar timeframe, Singapore Airlines grew to become the world's second-largest air carrier by dedicating itself to customer service.

"Too Big to Fail" is False: Giants Have Indeed Fallen

In the wake of ABCP (Asset-Based Commercial Paper) devaluations, several countries bailed out a selection of their largest companies. However, some giant financial institutions were allowed to fail, although of course other firms were rescued. Lehman collapsed[2] in September of 2008, disappointing those who believed that it would be rescued as Bear Stearns had been.

---

[2] "Why letting Lehman go did crush the financial markets", Sam Jones, Financial Times (of London) in March 2009, at http://ftalphaville.ft.com/blog/2009/03/12/53515/why-letting-lehman-go-did-crush-the-financial-markets/ .

The admission in May 2012 by JPMorgan Chase's CEO, James Dimon, that a $2 billion loss was "egregious" led to speculation that banking needs even stronger regulations than the still-upcoming "Volcker rule"[3]. This bank's derivative trading loss was due to "many errors, sloppiness and bad judgment", according to Dimon. Some American politicians, such as Rep. Barney Frank, seemed especially unsympathetic to the industry in the light of this news.

In late spring of 2012, The Times of India reported[4] that India was losing out on capital investments. As a member of the "BRIC" group of nations, (Brazil, Russia, India and China), India had seen an influx of foreign investments attracted to high return on investment in a country with a rising GDP. The Reuters report indicated a change from $13 billion in net investment during the first two months of 2012, to a net outflow of over half a billion dollars in March and April. International investments are instead flowing to the ASEAN (Association of South East Asian Nations) market.

The reasons for this shift in investor sentiment may be open to discussion. Rising inflation in India and strong growth in Indonesia might be recent changes. A lethargic or corrupt bureaucracy in India has been the subject of whispers for some time, so this should not bear all the blame. Perhaps the investment firms have taken note of plans for the ASEAN countries to form an economic free-trade union to ease access to natural resources and cheap labour. (Natural resources are spread throughout Indonesia; Singapore has financial institutions; some types of skilled labour are quite affordable in the Philippines). In any case, the changing investment climate might be an early sign of the Indian economic giant's fall.

The New Normal: Small is the New Big

The notion of "normal" does change. In prehistoric times, hunter-gatherers gave way to farmers and shepherds. Craftsmen and artisans were replaced by factories or foundries. A local butcher shop would be supplanted by a supermarket anchoring a mall.

---

[3] "JPMorgan's surprise $2 billion loss sparks calls for heavier regulation", Daniel Wagner, AP, May 11, 2012, at http://www.thestar.com/business/investing/article/1176717--jpmorgan-chase-loses-2-billion-because-of-sloppiness .
[4] Reuters, "As funds flee, India's pain is Southeast Asia's gain" in *The Times of India* on May 20, 2012 at http://timesofindia.indiatimes.com/business/international-business/As-funds-flee-Indias-pain-is-Southeast-Asias-gain/articleshow/13317960.cms .

Yet, the tide is turning back in some market segments. Craft beer is again served by local breweries. The "locovore" movement asks people to buy produce from local farmers. The term "hand crafted" denotes high quality, attention to detail and customization for the individual customer.

"Big" Had Been Glorious

Investors used to place a premium on "big". The larger the banking institution, the more secure it seemed. Producing and selling more cars proved the quality of those automobiles.

Especially in the United States, the fast food industry sold large portions to demonstrate "value" to individual consumers. The phrase "Supersize Me" only worked as a movie title because it was a common request when ordering French fries.

Larger cars had been popular when fuel was cheap. Add lots of chrome and tall fins so other people will notice how much you can afford.

The same mind-set permeates investors and business analysts. As a corporation grows, it increases its value to its shareholders, to the governments to which it pays taxes, and to its customers and employees. This premise can be false. Larger companies can and do fall into bankruptcy; find ways to avoid taxes; provide poor or uninspiring service; and terminate employees by the factory.

While some large corporations do well, it is also possible for them to do very poorly indeed.

"Small" Is Now Beautiful

Times have changed. Banks that were "too big to fail" either failed or required massive bail-outs. Manufacturing is moving from "mass production" to "mass customization". The most successful car makers build to order rather than building base models to be foisted on dealers who then try to convince their customers to buy what's on the lot.

As Greece leads the European Union through a fiscal crisis in the spring of 2012, one must ask "If a whole country can teeter on the brink of insolvency, can any corporation grow large enough to be invulnerable"?

Whether or not consumers actually try to eat less, the trend in fast food is moving toward healthier choices. Although we still want to eat well, we also value "smaller waistlines". The laws of physics dictate that, for the same aerodynamic shape and engine efficiency, a smaller and lighter car will use less fuel than a heavier model. A canoe has a smaller turning radius than an oil tanker. A single-prop bush plane can take off from a much shorter runway than can a Boeing 747.

Size matters; small can indeed be beautiful.

Small Ventures Can Make Profits

Small can also be very profitable. The first "Star Wars" movie ("Episode IV: A New Hope", as it was eventually subtitled) cost under $15 million in 1977 dollars, but set box office records. Of course this spawned sequels that cost far more to produce, but the franchise has been profitable through them all, particularly with revisions and re-releases in various formats and merchandise spin-offs.

Several small countries have found ways to compete with their larger neighbours. Singapore, Hong Kong, South Korea, and Taiwan have strong economies, despite the twin Goliaths of India and China in their region. Sweden sets the standard for hosting the largest number of multinational companies per capita. Part of their success is the network of partnerships among their universities, corporations, and small high-tech venture firms.

Will North Korea Emulate Singapore and Indonesia?

A question recently posed by The Times of India asks whether Singapore can serve as an economic model for North Korea[5].North Korea's parliamentary leader, Kim Yong Nam, and two other leading officials began a trade and economics mission to Indonesia in May 2012. While both the United States and the United Nations are imposing sanctions on North Korea for its ongoing rocket testing activities, this "rogue state" is seeking to improve its economy by forging business ties with several countries in its region.

---

[5] "Can Singapore serve as economic model for N Korea?", May 12, 2012 in "The Economic Times" of *The Times of India* at http://economictimes.indiatimes.com/news/international-business/can-singapore-serve-as-economic-model-for-nkorea/articleshow/13110813.cms.

Western nations have often considered North Korea to be a closed economy. In part, this is because of trade embargoes based on protecting South Korean interests or security. North Korea does conduct trade with Singapore, Indonesia, Thailand, and other countries in southeast Asia. North Korea also has "special economic zones", similar to Singpore's , to facilitate trade especially with China.

North Korea has plenty of cheap labour and a national goal of increasing the importance of light industry, including the manufacture of consumer goods. They are one of a very few countries able to export manufactured goods to China at a profit, because Chinese labour costs have escalated in recent years as this economy grew.

North Korea might import raw materials from Indonesia, or perhaps learn how to develop its own mineral resources from Indonesian companies. North Korea might be sitting atop natural resources worth trillions of dollars if they can be extracted and sold. That value might increase if these resources are processed locally and sold as consumer goods rather than as commodities.

The news article speculated that Singapore could provide several lessons to North Korea. Singapore's successes include wooing international investments, developing profitable low-cost manufacturing, and improving its economy while maintaining political stability and retaining its existing political structure.

The Beauty of Small Business

Small business also has its beauty. This goes beyond the push to "buy local", which may indeed reduce pollution from transporting goods across vast distances. It includes the way people value dealing with a local entrepreneur who knows his customers and will customize service. In part, this is about "improving the customer experience".

Craft breweries provide an example where small size is intrinsically linked to the main selling feature. A small number of mammoth companies, such as SABMiller and Anheuser-Busch Indev, brew hundreds of millions of barrels of beer every year. They may have facilities in many countries, but the business model relies on volume, brand recognition, and the strong market for reliably familiar taste. This leaves a niche for many single-site microbreweries, each catering to local consumers on the basis of flavour, quality ingredients, and local pride.

But the beauty of small business goes beyond a single consumer's experience. Small and medium enterprises have an economic importance far beyond what is usually credited to them.

The Social Value of Small Business: Overall Employment and Job Creation Rates

Large corporations may dominate the headlines in financial reporting. They may dominate the Dow Jones Index or the Hang Seng. Yet, statistics show that small businesses outperform conglomerates in several key metrics.

Overall Employment

Based on information released by the World Bank in 2011, which was based on reports from 81 countries over an 11-year period, small business dominated the employment numbers. Companies that employed 5-99 persons accounted for 65% of the workforce, whereas corporations with over 500 employees hardly registered on the graph.

Job Creation Rates

The World Bank also reported on job creation. Those companies with 5-99 employees created about 40% of the new jobs. Those with over 500 employees created about 15%.

Outlook on Capital Spending and Employment

John Tozzi[6] found that both the capital spending and employment outlook rates in large enterprises plummeted in early 2006, and then levelled out to be on par with small business rates. Starting about the middle of 2008, both metrics went into freefall before recovering a year later – but only for the big business respondents. During that time, small business outlooks declined only slightly.

---

[6] John Tozz,
http://www.businessweek.com/smallbiz/running_small_business/articles/small_business_economy/

Quiet Confidence

Gallup polls[7] from 2008-2010 have shown that about 60% of respondents had "a great deal" of confidence in small business; only about 20% felt the same about "big business".

Over the same time period, only 7% had "very little or no" confidence in small business. However, over 35% of respondents expressed "very little or no" confidence in big business.

These confidence numbers may or may not have an immediate effect on purchasing decisions. They do show, however, that the battle for the hearts of consumers may be all uphill for large corporations; they do not start from a strong position of trust.

The Internet is the Great Equalizer

A large corporation may feel compelled to advertise during the Super Bowl. The final championship game of America's National Football League is now known as much for the innovative commercials as for the half-time show or the quality of the sports competition. The cost to plan and produce an ad, and the price tag for airing it, add to the cachet.

Small businesses cannot hope to compete for the relatively few advertising minutes available for one highly watched television event such as the Super Bowl.

An alternative is to buy many more minutes of commercial time during many other programs, and to spend additional sums for radio, newspaper and magazine advertisements.

Fortunately, small businesses no longer need to compete for media advertising space; at least, not nearly as much as before.

Inexpensive Internet Advertising

The Internet is an incredibly inexpensive advertising medium. A small business can create a presence on the Web for a fraction of the cost of traditional media. Yes, creative ideas are still required and professional quality video should be produced: these will cost money.

---

[7] Gallup polls, http://www.gallup.com/poll/5248/big-business.aspx

Entertain and Inform

However, if the presentations are entertaining as well as informative, it is indeed possible to attract prospects and convert them into customers. In fact, the Internet is not merely "the latest and greatest" tool for marketing; it offers opportunities to reach out to, and engage with, both prospects and customers in a variety of innovative and creative ways.

One approach is to combine information, entertainment, and reader engagement in one site. This requires writing informative articles on subjects where the business has expertise. One possible example would be the hardware retailer with a series of articles on home repair projects. If the articles are well-written and authoritative, some people will read them for enjoyment or for the hints and tips. As well, both "brand awareness" and loyalty may be fostered by these articles. If a reader finds the need to repair something, her first thought for supplies should be that specific retailer.

Content Marketing

Current phrases that describe this approach are "content advertising" and "content marketing". These articles are not primarily advertisements in the classic sense that simply offer a product by listing benefits. Instead, content marketing provides useful background information so the prospective customer will be better informed.

An online insurance broker provides an example of successful content marketing. The primary service for this business is simply to collect information from a prospect, submit tentative applications to a variety of online insurance companies, and then link the prospect to the insurer providing the lowest quote. Whatever the technical challenges, the business model follows directly from the traditional broker who obtains quotes or simply refers to guidelines published by the insurers.

Yet the successful online brokers supplement their web sites with articles that inform their prospects about the insurance business. These articles lend an air of authority and trustworthiness to the site. In addition, the articles serve as "bait". People searching for insurance might find the article, rather than the application page. Also, these brokers place similar informational content on other site, along with a link to their brokerage site. Their articles reach new readers on the other sites and provide advertising for their business

Content marketing provides a free service to prospects, while attracting new business with authoritative and useful information.

Cultivate an Online Presence: Social Marketing via the Internet

Some portion of a company's "online presence" should reside on social sites, such as Facebook, Google+, and Twitter. Again, it will be important to assign staff to monitor these sites and respond to queries and comments. Consumers use these platforms to feel a personal connection with "their" brand; this feeling leads to repeat sales and brand loyalty. However, it does require dedicated human contact. A small business owner cannot devote all her time to posting updates, but should monitor the account, update regularly, and respond to direct queries within a reasonable timeframe.

An advantage for the small business using social sites is that the consumers appreciate that it is indeed the owner who is online with them and not a hired representative who has "no say" in running the business.

Another technique for small business is to write articles and advertisements that use a "long tail keyword". As an example, the phrase "bespoke tailor" has meaning for men who want a custom-tailored suit. Every tailor in the English-speaking world can use that specific phrase. However, "bespoke tailor in South London" and "bespoke tailor on Savile Row" are long tail keywords that specify the geographic location. Local customers often include geographical keywords when seeking a retail outlet. This is an advantage for the canny local retailer, who may only expect to serve the neighbourhood. Meanwhile, a national franchise might rely on the brand name, but cannot easily repeat the key phrase for each location across a country.

Make no mistake about it: the Internet levels the playing field, but it still costs something to enter the stadium.

Chapter 3 – HOW SMALL BUSINESS CAN CLIMB SEVEN MOUNTAINS

Most small businesses face seven giant obstacles or mountains. Here we will introduce tactics to help you climb these mountains.

Overview of Seven Specific Mountain-Climbing Tactics

Strategy provides high-level guidance and is vital for long-term success. However, short-term tactics are required to turn the strategy into a reality and climb the mountains or overcome obstacles before taking on the giant.

Seven tactics that a small business should consider for quick improvements that can continue to pay dividends throughout the life of any company are:

1. Negative mind-sets: Win the mind game.

2. Office politics: Fly above the fray.

3. Bottlenecks: Identify and demolish bottlenecks through transformation.

4. Loss of Focus: Identify and serve your market niche.

5. Blunt Knives: Identify and sharpen the right productivity tools.

6. Advancing to the Rear: Instead, innovate to outsmart your competition.

7. Paralyzed? Take action!

Tactic 1: Overcome Negative Mind-sets

The first mountain to conquer is a negative mind-set. This is a characteristic of those who see no safe solutions.

It is far too easy to accept a negative mind-set: "This plan is too risky; the competition is too intense; we should not even try". Although external enemies may be real, powerful and dangerous, one's own negative mind-set can cause defeat without a battle.

Conversely, having a positive attitude can empower individuals and energize teams. Xerox claims that its success is due, in large part, to fostering a positive mind-set among its employees.

If You Don't Shoot, then You Don't Score

Consider this aphorism from professional athletics: "You never score if you don't shoot".

Thomas Alva Edison tried hundreds of materials and methods when developing the light bulb. If he had stopped trying, he would not have succeeded.

Sales managers often note that trainees often have trouble closing the deal, even when the prospect has indicated being receptive to the proposal. A significant problem is a reluctance to ask for the decision to purchase. Using a question such as "Cash or credit?" or "When would you like it delivered?" is helpful, because it includes the assumption that the customer actually wants to buy the item. By putting the focus on a specific commitment related to the purchase, this helps to ensure that the decision is both positive and endorsed.

David's friend Jonathon, Saul's son, was a prince in Israel. He and his personal armour bearer went to scout out a Philistine garrison. Jonathon had planned to attack if the Philistine guard was so overconfident as to "invite" him to the garrison; this would be the sign that God would give him victory. If Jonathon had stayed safely behind his own lines, he would not have defeated that guard...and caused panic among all the encamped Philistines.[8] His courageous attempt led to a major victory. If he had not tried, he would not have succeeded.

Build a Positive Mind-set

Several steps can help a business manager to overcome a negative mind-set:

---

[8] I Sam. 14: 1-23 (King James Version).

1.   Schedule a regular time to brainstorm new tactics.

2.   Develop an objective tool to evaluate potential risks and benefits.

3.   Budget time and money for new projects.

Set aside a regular opportunity to "dream up" new opportunities. While most of these ideas will be impractical, some may have potential. The key is to "exercise the muscle" that is the mind.

Consistently use an objective tool that requires listing risks and rewards, costs and benefits. This permits a fair comparison and prevents negative emotions from making problems loom too large.

Yes, it is foolish to simply charge ahead with a bad idea. However, you are indeed capable of finding positive solutions. The proof is that you already are in the position to make those changes. Others have confidence in you; that's the start for your positive mind-set.

Chapter 10 explains how to develop a positive mind-set.

Resources for a Positive Mind-set

It is said that hard work and excellent skills fall short of complete success; but adding a positive attitude results in 100 per cent productivity. In any business success starts from the mind so any negative attitude greatly affects the business.

How to overcome a negative mind-set

•   Have faith in yourself and your abilities. This will give you the energy and morale to achieve your goals.

•   Look to your family and friends for support. They are the greatest source of moral and emotional support needed to achieve your goals.

•   Don't give up after failing. Instead use these failures as learning opportunities.

•   Be patient. Rome wasn't built in a day. Don't be frustrated if you don't get the expected results immediately. It will take time and hard work.

- Persistence works well with patience. Keep trying until you achieve your goals.

- Have confidence in what you do. Low self-esteem won't help you achieve a positive mind-set. Use "positive self-talk": remind yourself that you <u>will</u> tackle and accomplish the next task.

- For those who believe in God: trust in God. He is the only one who can take you to greater heights.

Tactic 2: Fly Above Office Politics

"Prepare for the knock and overcome the block".

The second mountain consists of office politics. The military refers to self-inflicted injuries as "friendly fire", although the situation is far from friendly.

In any company, some co-workers or business partners will try to "knock down" a peer, in an attempt to gain a promotion or controlling influence among stakeholders. The victim perceives this as an attempt to block his own success.

The path of wisdom is to protect oneself while remaining a team player. In general, long-term business success can only come through cooperative efforts. Those who do not yet appreciate this will, however, compete rather than cooperate.

Corporations sometimes create competitions when the intention was to foster cooperation. There is nothing so absurd as to award a "team building" incentive to an individual, rather than to her successful team. If it takes a team effort to achieve a goal, then ensure that the whole team reaps the reward for their success.

Even in the absence of formal competition, it is important for the small business owner to offer incentives or to share unusually large profits. Set the example by publicly praising your employee for your company's successes, and by providing real rewards beyond mere words.

David Battled a Second Giant: King Saul

Although Goliath was the famous giant in the Philistine army, David also faced a different "giant".

David, an Israelite, was a loyal servant to King Saul. Before stepping out to fight Goliath, in a "champion versus champion" battle, David needed permission from Saul. Saul granted it, although he was concerned that a boy like David was outmatched by the giant who had been a fighter since his youth.

Later, as David amassed further military victories for the Israelites, King Saul was disturbed to hear women singing "Saul hath slain his thousands, and David his ten thousands."[9] King Saul began to envy his overly successful general and eventually attempted to kill David because he was afraid the Israelites would rise up and make David their king.

In our day, office politics can be as dangerous to one's career as envy was to David's very life. One modern stereotype portrays a manager who steals credit from his subordinates for innovative proposals.

The story of Saul and David shows the danger inherent in taking too much glory away from one's superior. Later, David's general Joab showed much greater wisdom in this regard. David had sent Joab to lay siege to Rabbah, the Ammonite's capital city. When Rabbah was nearly ready to fall, Joab sent a message to David: "...encamp against the city, and take it: lest I take the city, and it be called after my name."[10] Joab was wise enough to ensure his king received the glory for this military success.

In our world, avoid negative office politics by amassing praise for your manager so that he will be promoted and bring you along.

Turn to chapter 11 for further pointers on overcoming office politics in a small business environment.

Resources for Overcoming Office Politics

Also known as workplace or organizational politics, office politics occur when individuals in an organization use power explicitly or implicitly to try and gain an advantage over their colleagues.

---

[9] I Sam. 18:7 (KJV).
[10] II Sam. 12: 28 (KJV).

Here are some ways to succeed in handling office politics:

• Be a team player. If you create the impression that you are a loner then everyone will tend to be against you. Cooperation always helps to defuse office politics.

• Respect other peoples' boundaries. Don't give the impression that you know more about someone else's work than they do.

• Listen to other peoples' opinions. Accept others' views, and even their criticism, with an open mind.

• Stay away from office gossip. Gossiping greatly fuels office politics. Don't indulge in it.

• Raise issues with management in private. Showing dissatisfaction in public does not do anything to improve relations in the office.

• Constantly develop and maintain relationships. Also known as networking, this helps you advance your career.

• Practice good and consistent work performance. Let your work speak for itself and you won't need to engage in office politics to advance yourself.

• Be flexible. Go with the flow. It helps to keep updated on important developments.

Tactic 3: Identify and Demolish the Bottlenecks through Transformation

Any situation where a process slows down or gets delayed is a bottleneck. Treat these bottlenecks as defects in the process: they are problems in need of long-term solutions.

Perhaps the first task is to actually notice the bottleneck. It is easy to accept "that's the way it is" in the absence of competitive pressure.

Schedule yourself to review different aspects of your business operations, with a view to eliminate inefficiencies or bottlenecks. Do you need to record sales information in different places for accounting, inventory, and commissions purposes? Consider buying a software package to integrate these functions. Are projects delayed because you need to order basic materials before starting? Calculate the trade-off for maintaining a minimum inventory, versus the extended turnaround time for your customers.

Root Cause Analysis

One approach in correcting defective manufacturing processes involves "root cause analysis".

Here is an example. The quality analyst measures a widget, finds it is 5% too long, and decides it must be rejected. The analyst then determines the root cause with a series of questions and answers. "Why is the widget too long"? "The grinding operation did not remove enough material". "Why did the grinder malfunction"? "It seems to be working properly, but the abrasive component had worn down". "Why was this abrasive worn down"? "It wears down during regular use". "What should be done to prevent this problem"? "We must either replace the abrasive on a schedule, or inspect it on a schedule and replace it when needed".

Another example is the recurring need for governments to bail out their largest financial institutions. Large corporations might fail slowly if they have structural problems such as unfunded pension obligations or innovative competitors. But for a sudden banking crisis, one really needs a corporate culture that lends, invests, or "hedges" recklessly in search of quarterly profits, rising dividends, and excessive bonus payments.

This root cause approach works with almost any problem that is large enough to be noticed in the first place. Why did the problem occur? What leads to the problem? How can the problem be avoided?

Refer to the second section of Chapter 5, "Use Transformational Processes in the Right Situations", for more insights into the Corporate Transformation methodology.

Resources for Overcoming Bottlenecks through Transformation

Companies need to identify and clear bottlenecks to productivity and innovation initiatives. The analysis and preparation for unforeseen circumstances will help facilitate implementation and action.

How Some Businesses Succeed in Transformation by:

- Having visionary turnaround executives. These are the people who drive transformation in businesses.

- Identifying what it is that ails the company. This is the first step in transformation. It ensures that current problems do not recur in the future.

- Applying comprehensive transformational techniques. This includes changing the corporate culture among other techniques.

- Treating the root of the problem and not the symptoms. This is because the real problem lies in the root.

- Strengthening the corporate immune system. This helps in effectively tackling future problems.

- Being action-oriented. This includes flexibility and taking quick action.

- There should be personal transformation in each and every member of the business. This can be achieved by enhancing positive mentalities among the employees.

Tactic 4: Identify and Serve Your Market Niche

The SWOT analysis is a useful tool for identifying a market niche that your company should pursue:

- Strengths: Identify your company's strong points.

- Weaknesses: Likewise, determine where you are weak.

- Opportunities: What opportunities are available?

- Threats: What threats await us in this market niche?

The sweet spot for a niche opportunity allows your company to use its strengths where the competition is weak. It avoids markets where you are weaker than your competitors. Opportunities arise when a market is emerging but has not yet been satisfied. Threats include known competitors; unreliable suppliers or supplies; fluctuations in demand; and external risks such as interest rate instability.

Of course, the SWOT analysis for an opportunity should then estimate the expected profitability. Will there be a capital cost for investment? Can your small business find economies of scale to reduce the cost of raw materials? What would be a fair price and is there a market at that price? Do you expect to sell at a discount to improve volume or to keep competitors at bay?

Niches can be selected by small companies, international conglomerates, or even economic regions. Europeans may look to Germany for manufacturing or Sweden for innovations in medical arts. Many companies in Singapore focus on the middleman role: to purchase wholesale from Chinese factories and resell to American consumers.

As Michael Treacy and Fred Wiersema argued in their book *The Discipline of Market Leaders*, "Those successful companies – the market leaders – excel at delivering one type of value to their chosen customers". Seeking and exploiting a niche is not an act of weakness or cowardice; instead it is a spear thrust through the heart of the competition. Sun Tze, in *The Art of War*, recommended that an army only bring its forces to bear where the enemy is weakest – preferably by deceiving the foe into defending some other location.

Resources to Identify and Serve Your Market Niche

A target or market niche can be defined as a relatively small and profitable section of the general market suitable for focused attention by a business. It is created when a business or a marketer identifies needs and wants in a certain area that is not being met by competitors.

These needs must have something in common to qualify as a niche, but that "something" might change over time. For example, North American supermarkets used to sell raw or packaged foods; now some also prepare meals in competition with take-out restaurants. At the same time, coffee shops have broadened their product line to include cans of ground coffee to compete with the supermarket niche.

If you target a local market, then advertise on local radio stations or in local newspapers. A web site can use "long tail keywords", such as "...in central Singapore" to focus attention on that region. Conversely, if you sell globally, the Internet is the most cost-effective way to reach everyone who can access the Web.

How to Target the Right Market Niche

- Keep yourself up-to-date. This is the best way of knowing the specific needs and wants that must be satisfied in a specific market niche.

- Learn what you can do for that specific market. The customers are most interested in what you can do for them.

- Use the most effective advertising media depending on which market subsection you want to target. This may depend on age group, geographical location, and gender, among other factors.

- Test the market first. This will help to get an intimate knowledge of the targeted market niche. It also helps to know the risks involved.

- Use aggressive marketing strategies. This entails marketing your product in as many ways as possible.

- Use Internet marketing services. This is especially important in a technological world as our current one where the Internet is the most popular method of communication across the globe.

- Develop credibility and trust with customers. This can be achieved through instantaneous product delivery and also consistent quality product delivery.

Tactic 5: Identify and Use the Right Productivity Tools

It is more important to identify what should be made more productive than to throw a productivity tool at some random process.

Normally this step follows tactic #3: identify the bottleneck before making an improvement. However, sometimes a problem cannot be recognized before the solution has been created. You wouldn't buy anti-virus software for your computer if you didn't own one. You wouldn't need shoe polish if you were barefoot.

On a more serious note, you may require professional advice to recognize the need for greater productivity. Ask your auditor if there are more efficient ways to ensure compliance and accuracy; or engage a manufacturing consultant about ways to reduce waste or to organize workflow.

Well-Directed Productivity Tools for Accounting

Let's use an accounting process as an example of improving one's aim over time. Back in the days of pencils and paper ledgers, productivity could be improved incrementally by:

- Replacing a manual pencil sharpener with an electric model.

- Placing this device in a central location in easy reach of the bookkeeping staff.

- Installing one pencil sharpener on each accountant's desk.

- Issuing mechanical pencils to the staff, so they don't need to sharpen pencils at all.

Later, in a slightly more modern world, we replaced the ledger books with computers and spreadsheets, but continued to have the bookkeepers enter details from paper transaction slips. An improvement to the central accounting system could handle large volumes of standard transactions. Still later, that system was integrated with the bookkeepers' personal computers, with much of the data downloaded from sales registers, so they only had to input a few adjustments or one-time variances.

A business that must record many transactions has a greater incentive to improve productivity in this field, compared to one that has very few.

In short:

- Identify the vital tasks that take the most time or cost the most to perform.

- Identify the productivity tool that is most useful for these current or near-future tasks.

- Identify and eliminate tasks that are not required.

Poorly Aimed Quality Control in Manufacturing

A manufacturer's customer has returned a shipment of one particular model of a product and claimed that many fail to meet the specifications. In response, the manufacturer immediately added a quality inspection step after assembly was complete, but prior to packing and shipping. Over time, this process was optimized to initially check for the most frequently-occurring defects.

While this reduces the number of returns from customers, and optimizes the final inspection process, it aims at the wrong target. Ideally, each manufacturing step should be made as error-proof as possible, and each intermediate product (or a sample of them) should be tested as it leaves each step. This would avoid the wasted time and material of continuing to work with a flawed item, and lead to corrective action before many defects had been processed.

Resources to Identify and Use the Right Productivity Tools

Consistently low productivity is one of the major signs that a business is in its death throes. But not all hope is lost. With a good action plan, after identifying the root of the problem, the business can turn around from this dire situation and start boosting its productivity.

• Use online marketing. In this age of global networking one has to recognize the power of internet marketing. It leads to a wider market translating into more sales, more profits, and hence, higher production.

• Determine what your objectives are, noting market opportunities and competitors' positions.

• Make short-term changes to product mixing, pricing, and marketing and note the market's response to them.

• Compare your organization's productivity measure against industry standards and your competitors.

• Always be on the lookout for new opportunities to expand as this will give you a chance to boost your production.

• Find another alternative to firing staff. Alternatives may include pay cuts or changing full-time employees to part-timers. Firing usually reduces morale of the other staff leading to lower production.

• Enhance communication, cost control, cash flow, and concentration. (The four Cs).

• Boost the organization's risk preparedness and disaster management. This is especially important in the event of natural calamities where the organization has to be ready to contain the damage and quickly recover from it.

Tactic 6: Innovate to Outsmart the Competition

An innovative upstart can carve a lucrative niche against current competitors, or revive a market that had died out. Television programming provides two examples.

Lively Competition in News

The evolution of the "24 hour news network" is an example of an innovation that came to dominate its niche. Previously, the American broadcast television networks (ABC, CBS and NBC) allocated specific hour-long news programs that competed against each other on the basis of quality or breadth of coverage. However, each network had a greater focus on their entertainment programming.

Ted Turner founded CNN as an "all-news" channel, using the medium of cable television. The initial target market was conceived as the business executives who could only squeeze a limited amount of television viewing into prime time: they arrived home too late for the "6:00 o'clock news" but went to bed before the "11:00 o'clock news recap".

Turner's CNN innovation led to many competitors who present continuous streams of news reports tailored to different consumer demographics.

Another change is the tendency to present a viewpoint in news reports; this is in contrast to the previous journalistic goal of "balanced" reporting. Critics may say that "network X leans toward left-wing liberalism, but Y presents to a conservative, right-wing agenda". From a business perspective, this may be seen as a way of capturing a loyal audience for specific advertisers.

Reviving the Talent Show

Another innovative upstart in television is the family of "audition elimination" talent competitions. "American Idol" is one of many "Country Idol" clones, but "Country's Got Talent", "X Factor" and "So You Think You can Dance Country" are others.

Decades ago, local stations might carry a "Talent Time" program, mainly to showcase local youths or children. These programs could operate on a low budget, but had a following because the shows featured people from the community.

How did the new talent competitions become successful when they have so much in common with the defunct "Talent Time" format? Perhaps the single greatest innovation was to allow the audience to vote by telephone, SMS text message, or via the Internet. The audience could then influence the outcome.

Although any one viewer's contribution is negligible, the format provided at least as much of a sense of "ownership" as any democratic election.

Consumers feel a similar sense of connection and influence by "liking and following" celebrities and product brands on Facebook or Twitter. Receiving brief updates connects the consumer; replying and receiving responses gives the impression of influencing the company or celebrity. Perhaps, fans feel even greater loyalty if they knowingly spend some money on the premium message services.

Surely the additional revenue streams that came from "1-866" telephone calls and premium text messaging helped with the profitability of this format.

Finally, the hosts and judges are either famous enough to draw viewers initially or become notorious for their on-air personalities.

Final Lessons from the Entertainment Industry

The entertainment industry has been recycling concepts for a long time. The above section discussed television without mentioning standard ploys like cartoon adaptations (such as "Star Trek"). Cinema has borrowed from television (and vice versa!), books, and video games.

All genres have sequels. The previous version proved that there had been an audience. The "trick" now is to retain the best features of the original, while adding a component that appeals to the current audience.

Resources to Outsmart the Competition

A business can't keep walking the same old path especially in an ever changing world. It will eventually become obsolete and irrelevant if there is no innovation.

Factors that boost innovation

- Company leadership should support innovation to provide the morale necessary for creativity.

- Make use of problem finders. These people identify problems then set out to correct them.

- Don't give up after a failed attempt at innovation. Instead use the failure as a learning experience to prevent future recurrence.

- Nourish and encourage creativity. This creates an optimum environment for innovation.

- The organization should provide resources to support innovators. This may include helping them further their training and development.

- Pursue both innovation and productivity to gain a competitive edge.

- Have a balance between flexibility and enforcement. This is achieved through rules and regulations.

- Implement innovation productively. This is what makes the difference between productive and unproductive innovation.

Factors hindering innovation

- Office politics is one of the biggest hindrances to innovation and creativity. This is because employees concentrate on outdoing each other and not bettering the company.

- Fear of failure due to past occurrences is a hindrance. Past failures should not be hindrances but rather stepping stones to something better.

- Publicly discrediting new innovations of your competitors. does more damage to the company more than to your competitors. This makes the staff think that the company is invincible.

- When you solely rely on tested and tried ideas and formulae, you miss the opportunity where part of the successful innovation lies in risk taking, walking off the beaten path.

- A lack of a good environment for creativity and innovation may be brought about by the management or even fellow employees.

- Lack of resources to support innovators may include lack of research facilities or even inadequate funds to conduct that research.

Tactic 7: Take Action

The most difficult step is the one not taken. It is all too easy to begin analyzing a situation, to plan possible tactics, but fail to act. This is sometimes called "the paralysis of analysis".

One approach is to acknowledge that the first step is indeed only the "first step". By admitting that further actions will be taken, one is relieved of the responsibility of mapping out the whole campaign before the first shot of the first skirmish.

Ready, Aim, Fire, Aim Again and Keep Firing

Prepare by choosing a worthwhile target. This could be an excessive cost, a slow process, or a marketing opportunity. The key is to choose a target with a significant potential return for a limited investment of time, effort, or cash.

Sketch out the plan of attack. Since a small business is nimble and responsive, the plan does not require the same degree of detail that a conglomerate requires in planning a global advertising campaign.

Then take the first action in the plan. Briefly evaluate the success of each step just before taking the next. After that, just "keep on keeping on" until you've won the battle.

Encouraging Prospects to Become Customers

Sometimes a sales presentation overwhelms prospects with too many options. Faced with a complex decision, the response is more likely to be "Let me think about it". This postpones the risk of making "the wrong" decision, at the cost of missing out on "a reasonably good purchase".

A wiser marketing strategy is to offer only two or three choices. Because the decision is simple rather than complex, most prospects feel greater confidence in their ability to choose well.

Treat Yourself as a Prospect

As a business manager, you should consider all your options. But if you find yourself postponing urgent decisions because there are too many options, try a strategy that will lead you to act rather than procrastinate.

One method is to list the available options, plus two others: "do nothing" and "investigate further". Then cross off the options that lead to the worst results. Often "do nothing" falls into that category. Only after reducing the list to the three best actions should you consider taking the "investigate further" route – and only for those three best actions. Set a deadline for completing the investigation and making that decision.

So treat yourself as you would a prospective customer: reduce the number of options so as to simplify the decision-making process. Then take decisive action when you have enough information about the remaining choices.

Resources to Take Action

In business therapy, the corporation need not only take action but also must ensure they take the right action.

How to succeed in taking the right action

• Do it at the right time. Even if it is the right action it has to be taken at the right time otherwise it will be of no help.

• Completely understand what the problem is in the business. This will aid in taking the appropriate action.

• Foster innovation and take risks. This has especially been of help in keeping Google in business.

- Have executives who are able to deal with risks as opposed to the textbook executives produced by business schools today.

- Access your risks, calculate your next steps, and tap into your resources. (ACT) This constitutes the meaning of right action in business.

- Know what your goals are. You can't perform an action without knowing what result you desire from the action.

- Avoid negative office politics. Office politics lead to decisions that only favor some individuals.

- Foster a strong and healthy corporate culture that can take the right action at the right time.

- Enhance communication within the business to completely understand all aspects of the business.

- Cultivate a positive mental attitude among all employees. This will greatly enhance collective decision-making in the business.

Reviewing the Seven Mountains

Please refer to Appendix I for some more questions and answers to help you review these seven mountains.

Summary: How to Conquer Seven Mountains

Replace negative mind-sets with positive ones. You are in your current position in the company because you have the necessary skills and experience. Be confident and use these skills.

Rise above office politics. Find ways to share your success without leaving yourself vulnerable to a back-stabbing colleague.

Identify the bottlenecks; then eliminate them. Investigate "why" a process is slow, drill down to the root cause, and fix it.

Identify and serve your market niche. Periodically take the time for a SWOT analysis. Be sure to verify this with your existing market or identify a new market.

The right productivity tools can provide a significant competitive advantage. Start modernizing with the process that is least efficient, takes the most labour across your company, and has a low cost of improvement. Manufacturers, for example, have a variety of techniques such as 5S or kanban that can improve a process without huge capital investment. The specific technique or tool must be chosen based on your company's current activities and market goals.

Innovate to outsmart the competition. In some cases, market research will show that there was a demand for some outdated product; it simply needs to be upgraded to meet current requirements. (The Apple "computer" company has become a raging success by upgrading its products before the competitors caught up with its previous model). Other types of innovation may be as difficult as creating a new type of service, or as simple as simplifying the sales, ordering, or payments systems for your customers' convenience.

Take action. Define a project with deadlines for research, planning, and development. Then follow up with specific actions.

Chapter 4 – THE ADVANTAGES AND DISADVANTAGES OF SMALL BUSINESS

Clearly a small business is different from a global enterprise. There are fewer employees, fewer storefronts, fewer languages spoken, and fewer currencies to convert. Cash flow and capital assets are lower. Yet "differences" are not always "disadvantages".

Advantages of a Small Business

A small business can make use of its natural characteristics to take a competitive advantage over its larger competitors. These advantages include quickness, flexibility, and accessibility.

The Smaller the Business, the Quicker it can Act

A small business can act or react more quickly than a large enterprise. In part, this is because fewer people need to be informed and trained. As well, the global corporation has long-term contracts and commitments, both internal and with suppliers and customers.

Consider a small manufacturer that decides to implement a Six Sigma quality initiative. The company may have only one shop floor, a dozen machines to calibrate, and two dozen front-line employees to train. One or two Six Sigma projects yearly may result in improvements to reliability and, therefore, profit margins for most of the company's operations. By contrast, a global enterprise may need a year to decide where to implement its first Six Sigma project and which executives will take the lead.

Smaller Businesses are More Flexible

A small business is likely to have fewer automated processes and fewer employee manuals. What it lacks in bureaucracy, it can achieve with flexibility.

As one example, a global enterprise may have a rigid policy regarding its raw materials inventory. "Only cut this chunk of metal when all five pieces can be allocated to five end products" is a reasonable rule for a company with hundreds of items in its order book. This rule is too restrictive when a product line is coming to the end of its life cycle. The production manager states the new requirement: "We only need two pieces because we're building the final two products". Yet, the computerized manufacturing resource program (MRP) could insist on waiting for three orders that will never be written.

In contrast, the small business might neither have nor need an MRP system; and the manager would not accept a delay in fabricating the final pieces when they are needed to meet the delivery schedule.

There is, of course, the risk that a flexible approach to problem-solving will lead to excessive risk-taking. This risk is mitigated by the expectation that a small business owner will have a greater personal knowledge of the risks, especially those related to the customers.

One complaint in a major corporation is that "Let's run it past the Legal Department" is the usual way to obtain a "Don't do it" response. The reason is that the in-house lawyers are unlikely to be rewarded when a risky decision is profitable; but likely to be blamed if they approve an action that does not succeed, or causes problems. The predictable result is that the global corporations become very averse to risk, and therefore miss out on opportunities that may be taken by smaller competitors.

Smaller Businesses are More Accessible to their Customers and Employees

By its nature, a large enterprise shelters its top executives from employees and customers. Perhaps the most ubiquitous example is experienced with a call centre. Can a retail customer get past the front-line telephone operator to speak to a supervisor or technician when required? How much more difficult is it to contact a manager or executive?

In the same way, the normal chain of command for employees goes through their supervisors and middle management. Without a formal process to pass suggestions or criticisms up the line, it is too easy for executives to be isolated and insulated.

By definition, the small business owner is much closer to the front line. Indeed, some customers may value that contact so much that they are willing to pay a premium for the experience. The small business owner may earn greater loyalty from their employees than any large corporation could expect. This can turn into an advantage in terms of the employee's commitment to a project or to customer satisfaction.

Greater accessibility also paves the way for more innovation. It is easier for management to learn what the customers want in the next generation of products, simply because there is less insulation to keep the information from bubbling to the top.

Remember what was said about "long tail keywords" for greater success in Internet advertising. Include your location in describing your product or service. Examples include "...the finest product in city"; "...attentive service in local neighbourhood"; or "...delivering product in the region".

The Disadvantages of Being a Small Business

As Sun Tze said in *The Art of War*, it is important to know your enemy and yourself; then choose the right place and time to win the battle that hardly needs to be fought. The small business must know itself, including its own weaknesses. Let's consider the disadvantages that small businesses endure, and how these can be mitigated.

Small Business Lacks "Economy of Scale"

One disadvantage for small businesses is the lack of economy of scale. Large businesses can buy in bulk, ship in economical quantities, or manufacture a large run of products without changing the tooling setup.

Manufacturing Economy of Scale

The pursuit of large-scale efficiency can be a trap for a small business. The ideal scale would seem to require that every machine and person is fully loaded with work. The following illustrates this approach.

In China, one pig farmer worked to expand his operation for economy of scale. He had a number of employees and wanted to ensure that his equipment was fully utilized. He noticed that a tractor was idle for part of the day; let's say 10%. If he added the right number of pigs to the barn, that tractor would be fully occupied all day. To make that change, however, he would need an additional pump to deliver feed to the new pigs. However, that pump would be idle for part of the day. Adding yet more pigs would keep the pump busy, at the cost of an extra grain bin; that bin would have yet more capacity, so he needed more pigs again. Eventually, he needed to buy a larger farm for the extra barns and crops. Eventually, his expansion plans were quashed by concerns over the amount of liquid manure the pigs would produce next door to a tourist attraction.

In addition, the production schedule must include time for preventative maintenance and repair for equipment. One mitigating approach for the small business is to use a smaller machine, if possible, so it will work at a higher percentage of its capacity.

Employee training is another overhead that is more difficult to absorb in a small business, and especially difficult if the workers are fully loaded with work. However, training may be as important to employee retention and a competitive stance as preventative maintenance is for industrial equipment.

A small business needs reliable Internet access; it may not need a raised-floor server room to achieve this. (A locked room and a small uninterruptable power supply might be a good investment, however). In fact, the company might have almost no hardware at all, since the website could be hosted by a service provider. The necessities are: a great product or service, the website to present that product, and a comprehensive marketing plan.

Economy of Scale in Order Quantities

Wal-Mart is a prime example of a company that orders in bulk, demands discounts, and requires its suppliers to take responsibility for many intermediate processes. Wal-Mart can do so because of its purchasing volume. In the same way, it is more efficient to deliver a bin, barrel, or shipping container full of paper clips to a single customer than to deliver small boxes by courier to thousands of purchasers.

The small business might achieve some economy of scale by purchasing certain commodities in bulk. Such purchases require careful consideration. A carton of photocopier paper will probably not spoil; but will pre-printed letterheads be used before the company decides to use a new logo or moves to a new location? The same question applies to business cards: 1,000 may cost little more than 100, but will they be distributed before something changes?

Naturally, the cost of tying up capital in bulk purchases is another deterrent to economical ordering by small businesses. A small business might find consolation where it does not need to buy in bulk. One supplier may have an economical order quantity that would preclude a re-order for several years. Why would the small business want to tie up so much money in inventory?

At the same time, even the largest manufacturers are shifting to just-in-time inventory management and therefore are adjusting their order patterns. Rather than accepting a few large shipments, they insist that their suppliers deliver smaller quantities on a more frequent, "as required" basis. This saves on the cost of storing the raw materials and reduces losses due to rust or other spoilage. If this is a good idea for larger companies, it is an excellent one for small business.

Small Business Lacks Certain Resources

Major corporations can afford resources that small business owners can only dream of obtaining:

- a marketing team able to run focus groups and test campaigns in each target market;

- engineers working full-time on research and development;

- the most sophisticated equipment; and

- experts in every field are retained on the payroll.

Regarding these resources, the guideline for small business is to focus on what it needs, rather than on what it cannot afford.

The small business might not have a global market; why should it envy those who do? The key is to intimately know the current local market. Testing a new product or advertising campaign in the local market is relatively inexpensive, particularly if the population is fairly homogeneous. (A city with ethnic diversity due to immigration may present a larger challenge, but at least the market research firm does not need to travel to find test participants).

Unless the primary mission of the small business is research and development, there are far fewer risks in using available techniques and technology. "Why reinvent the wheel"?

Any company, large or small, that invests in equipment takes the risk that it will become obsolete before it has been written off by the accounting department. One approach for the small business is to rent or lease equipment that may outlive its usefulness. This may free up capital and certainly retains the advantage of being able to upgrade with less pain. Particularly in the "rust belt" of the United States, larger steel mills have been outgunned by smaller mini-mills with newer, more efficient smelters and a tighter focus on specific profitable products.

Small companies cannot retain expertise in every area, even when that expertise may be vital to profits or growth. One solution is to rent expertise. Consultants may cost more per hour than employees with similar qualifications. Yet their cost per annum is much less, if they are only brought in when required. There are also savings on benefits and the overhead involved in recruitment. As was noted already, the small business has an advantage in the area of training and learning: fewer employees need to be taught Lean Manufacturing practices, so a short-term project with an outside consultant might be sufficient.

Lacking Leverage

Unavoidably, small businesses cannot exert the leverage of large orders on their suppliers. They are unlikely to be the sole source of products for their customers. Banks are unlikely to allow a small business to leverage their property, inventory, or receivables to the same degree as a multinational corporation.

Small order quantities can be turned to one's advantage. First, the supplier should not require a long lead-time. This allows the small customer to shop later in the planning cycle, seeking clearance sales. Second, the small customer might institute just-in-time purchasing, thereby saving on storage costs and improving cash flow.

As a seller, the small business might strive to become the most responsive supplier for its customers. It might offer customization for special requests or quicker turnaround on standard orders. If it focuses on local customers, the small business might save on shipping costs or simply offer quicker delivery times.

Bookcase Study: Borders Group

Bibliophiles have observed bookstores battling for market share. The story of Borders Group is both a compelling history of success and a cautionary tale of failure.

A Brief History of Borders Group

Two university students, the brothers Tom and Louis Borders, sold used books in a small retail space. They expanded within their first decade, operated their own stores, and also managed inventory for affiliated but independent retailers. Throughout the first two decades, part of their growth came by acquiring other bookstores.

After two decades, Kmart bought Borders for its expertise in retail bookselling. The intention was to use Borders managers to guide Kmart's Wallenbooks division, which had a retail presence in shopping malls. Eventually, Kmart divested itself of its Borders-Wallen book division.

Borders Group expanded internationally, despite pressure from other successful "brick and mortar" book retailers such as Barnes and Noble. Borders Group's expansion included franchise stores as well as wholly-owned retail establishments. They also arranged for sales in the Starbucks subsidiary, Seattle's Best Coffee. They sold stationery under the Paperchase label. The dominant Internet retailer, Amazon.com, handled online sales until Borders launched its own e-business web site.

At its peak, Borders Group operated over 1,200 retail outlets and earned revenues in excess of two billion dollars. However, they stopped being profitable after 2006. In 2011, after forty years in business, Borders Group closed its remaining stores and re-routed its online customers to Barnes and Noble.

Analysis of Borders Group

The Borders brothers began as small a business as one could imagine: two partners selling used books in a small store. Early in their expansion, they used technology to their advantage with an inventory system that pushed inventory to the stores where it would sell quickest.

They made the most of many opportunities, showing flexibility in mixing self-owned bookstores, franchise operations, and store-within-coffee-shop business models. They partnered with Amazon as their online marketing agent. While some of their growth was by acquisition, they also grew organically by reinvesting profits.

They did react to signals that problems were looming. They shut down unprofitable or marginal stores. By taking online sales into their own site, they saved on sharing sales revenue with Amazon. They found new investors to keep the company afloat for a few years. They added a rewards program to foster customer loyalty, and worked hard to make the book-buying experience pleasant. They brought in new CEOs. They began to compete directly in the e-reader and e-book marketplace. At the end, a hoped-for buyout did not materialize to salvage their brand name.

Perhaps their undoing was due to a perfect storm: overall book sales declined as the economy shrank; e-books replaced "dead trees" as e-readers became more available; and of course, both Amazon.com and Barnes and Noble are formidable competitors.

On the other hand, the Borders brothers cashed in when they sold their business to Kmart in 1992. They made their capital gains, and the brand enjoyed both growth and success for about 35 of its 40 years in existence. The Borders Group is a bankrupt company today.

Summary: Advantages and Disadvantages of Small Business

A small business has several advantages over a global enterprise. The small company may be quicker to act or react, more flexible in its business arrangements, and maintain closer contact with its customers.

Of course, a major corporation can exploit economies of scale in purchasing or setting optimal production batch quantities. It may hire specialists in current and planned fields of endeavour. Finally, it can influence both customers and suppliers based on its size.

However, a small business can analyze and mitigate its disadvantages, or exploit its natural advantages, at least, within its chosen market.

The story of David and Goliath is instructive here. Both Goliath the Philistine soldier and King Saul of the Israelites expected that David would fight as a regular foot soldier. Saul provided David with armour and a heavy sword; but David had no experience with that gear and refused to use it. Instead, David relied on his shepherd's weapons: a staff and a sling with rocks[11]. By using his own tactics rather than Goliath's, David succeeded where any regular soldier would have failed.

---

[11] I Samuel 17.

Chapter 5 – STRATEGIES FOR SMALL COMPANIES

Overview: Three Strategies

Three strategies for survival and growth offer the greatest value to small businesses.

1.   Target and exploit the correct niche.

2.   Use transformational processes to correct current problems and lay the foundation for future growth.

3.   Implement programs to blend innovation and efficiency.

A small business might already be applying some of these techniques without using the labels. Adopting the required strategies will help any small business succeed.

First Strategy: Target and Exploit the Correct Niche

We have already noted that a small business lacks the resources to do everything or to be everywhere. Instead, as Sun Tze also advised, a small army can win territory if it chooses the correct location: where the enemy is weak or absent.   In business terms, this means choosing a niche with a competitive advantage. This may be a customized product, a unique service, or the use of local knowledge.

Chapter 6 explains more about the niche strategy.

Second Strategy: Use Transformational Processes in the Right Situations

The "Corporate Transformation" process was developed for major corporations, but is also applicable to small businesses. The full transformational process applies three phases in sequence, although the first phase is only appropriate to rescue a company from near bankruptcy.

The three stages are:

- "Surgery": emergency treatment to avoid bankruptcy by immediately improving cash flow.

- "Resuscitation": revive the patient after surgery with a focus on increased sales.

- "Nursing Therapy": develop a corporate culture which is fast, flexible, and innovative to avoid a relapse.

Sample Situations that Require Transformation: Globalization, Tribal Marketing, Word of Mouth, and Social Media

A company may require the transformational process due to difficulties caused by internal conditions or external situations. A business that loses track of receivables while pursuing sales, for example, causes own cash flow problems. A retailer might be threatened by the news that Wal-Mart is about to open shop in her small town; this is an external situation.

Small manufacturers in Western countries are under siege by globalization: China can produce almost any physical product at a very competitive price. How should a company respond?

One might advertise through local newspapers or flyers. The costs are fairly high and the results may be spotty or difficult to measure. How can a business utilize "tribal marketing" to reduce expenses and focus on the target market? Can a small business generate sales through word of mouth? Can it make use of social media?

Chapter 7 explains the Transformational Process and the above situations in greater detail.

Third Strategy: Productive and Innovative Implementations

Twin pillars for every successful company are to innovate productively and to improve productivity through innovation.

Attention to productivity means that you can manufacture more goods with greater efficiency and this leads to improved profits. Unfortunately, it also leaves your company vulnerable to new innovative solutions from your competitors. There was no point to making Betamax video systems more efficiently once the VCR format had overtaken the market.

However, a continual focus on innovation means that each product is a prototype, leaving no room for improved productivity. Since few companies can afford to invent a new solution for each project, this can be a quick route to bankruptcy.

Chapter 8 resolves the dilemma of Productivity versus Innovation.

Chapter 6 – STRATEGY #1: DETERMINE AND EXPLOIT THE NICHE

An entrepreneur need not be ashamed that her business only carries a few products in a local market. Even multi-national conglomerates may need to focus on their own niche, rather than scattering its investments and efforts too broadly.

A small business may have fewer choices than a large enterprise, but two decisions are vital:

- In which niche should it compete?

- How can it exploit that niche?

Even Conglomerates May Need a Niche

A small business must begin by determining its first niche. Success comes by exploiting its advantages in that niche.

There is one "niche" that every business, from the self-employed entrepreneur to the largest conglomerate, should target: to provide something of value to the customer while honouring professional ethics and the laws of the land. All people and businesses have "noble" responsibilities regarding ethics, environmentalism, and the way individual employees, suppliers and customers are treated. Unfortunately, these statements are too broad to guide a tactical plan of action. Few of us can be "all things to all people". Some large corporations have been chastened for excessive diversification.

In "Warren Buffett: Why the oracle of Omaha is irrelevant", the *Toronto Star's* David Olive criticizes Berkshire Hathaway for, among other things, running "70-odd operating businesses". In contrast, Olive cites United Technologies Corp. as a "focused conglomerate" where each subsidiary shares critical features. This company exploits a "niche" with clientele able to pay handsomely for products featuring intense Research and Development.

It is easier for a small business to retain its focus on its niche, since it lacks both the capital and human resources that permit seeking every pot of gold under every rainbow. Yet temptations may arise: to follow every potential lead; to pursue every income opportunity; or to expand before becoming successful in one location. Perhaps the greatest danger is an entrepreneur who can sense opportunity but lacks the discipline and focus to make one fortune rather than pursuing many.

In early 2012, the Canadian business press detailed how Research in Motion (RIM) struggled to maintain market share in the smartphone space. While RIM had begun to penetrate the consumer market with its Blackberry mobile phones, its competitors' consumer products were becoming acceptable for business users. By the end of March 2012, RIM had begun to reposition the Blackberry primarily as a business solution. Retrenching from its excursion into "a smartphone for all consumers" to more defensible market segments (possibly including part of the consumer space) may yet salvage RIM's future in its niche market. By the end of June 2012, Canadian analysts began saying that, if RIM fails to introduce its next device before the pre-Christmas shopping frenzy, it will have completely lost its competitive edge. That reasoning certainly would apply to consumer goods. It does not take into account the business market, but the workplace trend to "bring your own device" might put the nail into RIM's coffin.

A Niche is Not a Fortress

Although developing your own niche is a good strategy, this does not transform your business into an impregnable fortress. One business model under severe attack is the traditional large-scale supermarket for groceries. After decades of successfully defining and defending their niche, they now face serious competition from Wal-Mart.

A single Wal-Mart store might serve as an example of the "focused conglomerate". It sells a huge variety of goods from one location, but each product line is targeted to its niche. The common feature is the impression of offering low prices. Many customers accept the value proposition that they can make one trip to buy everything on their shopping list. This leads these consumers to shift loyalty for groceries from the traditional supermarkets to the "big box" stores.

However, some supermarkets use a similar ploy to lure other customers away from specialty grocers or butchers. One tactic is to define an "in-store delicatessen" or other high-end mini-store inside the main space. Meanwhile, local grocers and butchers continue to provide specialty items; they tend to focus on having a convenient location, superior quality, or a unique assortment of foods in inventory.

The lesson here is to begin by developing a niche for a specific type of customer. Ensure that your marketing promotes the distinctive and unique values your brand provides to those customers.

Google Created Many Niches

Google acts as a prime example by creating and filling multiple niches. In its infancy, Google's primary task was to present "Internet search results". By typing a few keywords into the Google search page, a user would quickly see a list of the web pages that used those words. This was much faster than the original Yahoo! method for which the user had to navigate a hierarchy of menu items to find the appropriate list of web sites. Soon other companies, including Yahoo!, began to offer similar services.

Whether it invented searching for "images" or street addresses, or acquired companies that did so, Google expanded its "search" offerings into various new niches.

Google also found a way to monetize its primary product by selecting and presenting advertisements based on the same keyword selection used to find the appropriate web sites.

By offering the AdWords, AdSense, and Analytics products, Google created ways for advertisers and publishers to share and understand the advertising revenue stream, thereby encouraging participation. Google's "Keywords for Search" helps writers decide what phrases might be most profitable in an online article.

Google also competes in almost every popular niche available on the Internet, with services for e-mail, document storage and sharing, calendars, video storage (by purchasing YouTube), a news feed, a calendar, a blogging platform, the Chrome browser, and the Google+ social network – to name only a few. Google will probably make this list out-of-date by the time this book is published. Outside the Internet, Google is associated with developing the Android cell phone operating system.

Google has been criticized for previous attempts to "do social"; the "Buzz" approach failed to achieve success. On the other hand, they continue to pursue this niche, which is gaining in popularity and may challenge the company's traditional foundation as a "search" engine.

Google has grown by acquisition as well as by developing new software and services to create new niche markets for itself. The moral of the story is that Google is not just a Goliath of the web; it also acts as an army of Davids, competing in a variety of niche markets but cooperating with each other to better understand their users.

Multiple Niches at Yahoo!

Although the official name may be "Yahoo!", the exclamation mark is too annoying to use consistently.

Yahoo is the other big-name Internet search engine in the Western world, with its own history of building innovative niches.

Yahoo's Origins

Founded by Jerry Yang and David Filo in 1994, the original "Yahoo" web site was not a search engine. Instead it was a directory, constructed as a hierarchy of categories that would lead to web sites. To find the "New York Yankees", for example, one might have started with "Sports", then make further selections for "Team Sports", "Baseball", "Professional", "United States", and "Major League Baseball" to find the list of MLB teams' web sites.

One advantage of using a hierarchy, rather than a search, is that the user is more likely to find the correct result, although at the cost of making extra choices. A person searching for "Yankees" with the intention of finding web sites devoted to American history now finds that most of the suggested results deal with professional baseball. Searching through a hierarchy from "History" through "American" would avoid the baseball sites.

Yahoo's Niches

Yahoo now offers a search facility rather than a hierarchical index. Yahoo added a "portal" page, with links dedicated to its favoured sites, in the hope that its users would open their browsers to this portal. By providing further self-branded services such as e-mail and specialized news feeds, the goal is to serve more advertising and keep its users from visiting rival sites.

The portal page is customized according to the country from which the user is browsing. This should mean that both the news and advertising contents suit the interests of the user. Teaming up with ISPs such as AT&T supports the promotion of the Yahoo portal as the default home page.

From its portal, Yahoo offers news in various categories, such as "Finances", "Movies" and "Music". There are lifestyle and health pages, celebrity gossip pages and the ubiquitous weather forecasts. Beyond e-mail, other services include job postings and telephone directory look-up. Yahoo also offers news apps for the iPhone, and "daily offers" for shopping. The contents of Yahoo's linked pages might be obtained from outside sources, but the user is unlikely to be concerned. Yahoo's pages are monetized with advertising.

Beyond the portal and its related content, Yahoo offers other Internet services such as web hosting. These services are comparable to what other Internet Service Providers (ISPs) supply, from small basic sites with e-mail accounts through large e-commerce emporia.

Like Google, Yahoo will also present advertising on web pages and share the revenue with those publishers.

Yahoo's Lost Opportunity with GeoCities

One of Yahoo's early acquisitions was GeoCities. Like Yahoo, Geocities was organized as a hierarchy. However, each virtual "city" represented an interest group, such as cinema or finance. Perhaps the most important feature, which was innovative at the time, was the facility for users to make their own web sites within the GeoCities landscape, at no cost to the user. This foreshadowed the Web 2.0 practice of creating and hosting blogging sites where users store their own creative content.

GeoCities grew its base of committed content providers and readers. It was a very popular site with significant traffic. Unfortunately, it was more of a popular hobby than a profitable business.

In retrospect, Yahoo mismanaged its GeoCities business, by making changes that were not appreciated by the existing user base. For example, Yahoo tried to appropriate all the user-provided content by claiming the copyright on everything posted in GeoCities. In response, many users left GeoCities. Today, many modern blogging sites explicitly acknowledge that the original writer or content provider retains copyright to those materials.

Later, in an attempt to profit from its significant acquisition investment, Yahoo offered a premium version of the GeoCities service. The remaining free service had limits on data storage and data transmission. This had the effect of "punishing" those who had the most loyal and active followings, or who posted the most content. Apparently GeoCities never did earn its keep for Yahoo, which closed this service (except in Japan) in 2009.

Yahoo's Problem in Providing Niche Services

Despite its longevity and the breadth of services that it offers, Yahoo is seen as an also-ran rather than as a leader. It had a head start on Google, which publicly began its search business in 1998.

Yahoo wisely switched from the hierarchical directory model to a search model, as it became clear that people preferred to type a few keywords in the hope of finding a reasonable result with one press of the "Enter" key. As well, while everyone needs to spend some time learning to use any system effectively, once one learns to use a search process, the methods apply to any keywords. Conversely, after learning how to use a hierarchical index, one must still learn the correct path to find each new subject.

The use of key words also makes it easier to serve relevant advertisements, since the search engine knows what the user is looking for. Simply following a hierarchy does not provide as much insight for the advertiser.

Yahoo pursued a variety of business opportunities, as did many other Internet companies. For example, once a company has built and maintained its own data centres in different countries, it should be relatively simple to offer domain hosting and other ISP services to others. Once one hosts user sites, it should be straightforward to offer premium upgrades or to create self-branded news or opinion sites.

Any one niche can be successful. Even if Google has a commanding lead in the number of publishers who monetize their web sites with Google's advertising, there should be room for a lower-cost second-ranked alternative ad server.

Why then is Yahoo not known as the leader in any niche and often not even as the second-best alternative?

It is truly difficult for an outsider to point to one root cause. However, there are several obvious effects. By the middle of 2012, Yahoo's board had spun through three CEOs over a three-year period. If the

Page 62

board members did share a unified vision, they have not been able to find a top executive who could achieve it. In CNN Money, Julianne Pepitone noted that recent CEO Scott Thompson tried to address the "central question of just what Yahoo is, exactly"[12]. She reported that Thompson had begun reorganizing Yahoo into consumer, technology, and regional content groups.

Yahoo's board had famously refused a $44 billion buyout offer from Microsoft in 2008. Three years later, its market capitalization was about half of that offer. Given similar stock market performances in another company, some activist shareholders would clamour for a break-up or spin-off of high-value divisions.

Three problems stand out.

First, Yahoo does a reasonable job in many niches. Google tends to be the absolute leader in some niches and Yahoo seems to want the same success. Perhaps Yahoo should be content to do well enough in several niches, rather than to supplant Google in them.

Secondly, Yahoo pursues too many marginal opportunities. Where Google has a lot of cash to spend on diversified projects, but is willing to cut them when they fail, Yahoo has a smaller war chest and must reap major successes in order to cover the varied expenses.

Third, Yahoo has copied many existing Internet business models: search engines, content publication and syndication, and web hosting have been named. Each of these markets is strongly contested. Yahoo is unlikely to dominate any of these areas.

My advice for Yahoo would be to focus on core competencies and accept that it has missed the opportunity to be the dominant player in any of its current markets. It should spin off the marginal divisions, at least to reduce expenses. Yahoo must then plan a strategy to be the first to enter an emerging market. Conversely, it could buy a rising new star, much as it did GeoCities; but it needs to understand how that start-up company had achieved its early success. Finally, any such new endeavour must include a plan for earning a profit, rather than simply growing market share.

---

[12] Julianne Pepitone, "Yahoo's CEO is out. Now what?", CNN Money (May 15, 2012) at http://money.cnn.com/2012/05/15/technology/yahoo-future/index.htm .

Determine the Correct Niche

What criteria determine the niche to be pursued? Consider the following:

- Start with opportunities in the local market.

- Start with proven expertise.

- Research the market for what is currently profitable and has the potential for growth.

- Consider what can be customized by your small business but not by a conglomerate.

- Consider expanding to related niches as your capabilities grow.

Opportunities in the Local Market

As it begins operating, a retail business might expect to operate from a local storefront. Ask "Are there potential customers in this area already?"; "What product or service is needed here?"; and "Is no-one already fulfilling this need"?

It is difficult to notice a potential customer if no one is already meeting the need. Indeed, a marketing study may have trouble convincing anyone of the need. Therefore ask "Is the need being fulfilled by an out-of-town provider"?

Perhaps there truly is no market, at the present time, for what you hope to provide. Perhaps that is why you cannot identify an incumbent competitor. Is this a successful business in other regions? Do your potential customers share the characteristics with those who already buy the product elsewhere? Should you start by creating awareness and by educating your prospects about the service you plan to provide?

Other local opportunities arise because an existing business, whether small and local or a multinational conglomerate, is failing to satisfy its customers.

Exploit Proven Expertise

The business should begin with the expertise of the owner or manager. Should a condo-dwelling insurance salesperson start a lawn maintenance company simply because there is a need? It is possible, if the right operations manager can be hired; but it does not seem to be a natural fit.

Current Income and Potential for Growth

There is no point starting a business that has limited potential for income or growth. Although it may be personally fulfilling to teach others how to raise honeybees, there may be limited interest in your area. A small cost-conscious retail store might do well in a town too small for Wal-Mart; but they are significant competitors for any retailer whose customers are willing to drive to the nearest outlet mall.

Customization is the Ultimate Competitive Advantage

Finally, seek a niche that offers customized service. The personal care industry has many small barber shops, hair salons, and spas because their customers want to deal with familiar and trusted individual service providers. A hardware store can customize "knowledgeable advice" almost as readily as a construction contractor. A local realtor must know a few neighbourhoods intimately. Knowledge of local conditions cannot be matched by a national realty firm unless it hires local experts.

Starbucks is a leader in customizing the American coffee "experience". Their patrons order from a basic menu – coffee – but the size, type of brew, and additional ingredients make each cup different and distinct. The customer pays for the sense of being accommodated and pampered with the small luxury of a personalized cup of coffee. Starbucks, in turn, is expanding rapidly and gaining market share.

Modern Efficient Customization

Several modern manufacturing companies specialize in efficient customization.

In the distant past, each manufacturer relied on craftsmen to build each product by hand. Later, standardized parts allowed the assembly line to be manned by people with less skill. Each had to add a few pieces to the assembly, but they did so all day and every day. It became time consuming to change the tools in order to build a different product, so large batches became the most economical.

With the advent of computer-controlled machinery, it became possible to manufacture a single item almost as efficiently as a large batch of items. The most efficient car manufacturers now think in terms of "each batch is one car" and "each car is one batch", rather than considering a production run of thousands of cars, with identical trim and options, as a single batch.

An emerging manufacturing niche is to produce custom products to the customer's specifications.

A retail customer may order "custom window blinds and drapes" to fit their home's windows. Custom roll-up garage doors are available for companies that house outsized snow removal or earth-moving equipment, or even for home garages. Kitchen cabinets can be made to order, based on the size of the room and the desired type of wood.

The key requirements include: scalable plans for excellent initial products; investment in the skills and equipment to support customization; and a marketing plan to target those who need customized products at a mass-market price.

Carve a Niche Between Two Giants

In June 2012, Microsoft announced that it was developing the "Surface" tablet computer. This would directly compete with Apple's iPad tablets, particularly as Microsoft would build the hardware as well as supply the Windows 8 operating system.

One manager of business development for technical firms, Matt Assay, provided a brief analysis[13] of the new competitive landscape. He said that, while Microsoft and Apple could compete in the premium priced markets of the First World, the real winners would be the many programmers writing applications for Android devices.

He reasoned that Microsoft and Apple would compete head-to-head for the established market for high-priced, premium quality mobile devices. However, the growing market is in Brazil, Russia, India, and

---

[13] Matt Assay, "Microsoft's Surface plan means the world belongs to Android now", The Register, June 26, 2012, at http://www.theregister.co.uk/2012/06/26/brics_love_android/ .

China: the "BRIC" countries where many consumers are still adopting their first or second cell phone, smart phone, or tablet computer.

These markets demand low prices – lower than what Apple or Microsoft might accept to maintain their accustomed profit margins. Therefore, the lower price for Android devices would continue their dominance in the BRIC markets.

Another interesting feature of Microsoft's strategy is that it will compete with the hardware manufacturers who currently load a Windows operating system onto their mobile products. Will those companies switch to a Linux operating system, rather than compete with their former software vendor?

Whether Assay's reasoning is correct or not, his analysis applies for any small business facing big-name competitors. Carve out a niche that your industry giants overlook. When Microsoft and Apple clash for premium products, they leave a niche for entry-level goods. When supermarkets carry highly processed foods from industrial-scale agricultural conglomerates, and compete on price based on economies of scale, then premium organic produce becomes a desirable alternative for some shoppers. Big-box department stores carry many items; carve a niche by knowing your customer's preferences or adding value with advice, free delivery, or after-sales service and support.

How to Exploit the Correct Niche

Obviously this book cannot offer specialized advice to every business with details for operating successfully in every niche. These basic principles do apply:

- Write and reference your mission statement.

- Conserve and pursue cash.

- Advertise to your target market.

- Differentiate your product with service.

- Deliver excellent value to your customer or client.

The Mission Statement

Large companies may produce a mission statement in the way elephants produce baby elephants: with a great deal of high-level effort at the beginning, and a long gestation period before results are seen. While this may seem to be a joking attempt to dismiss the process, at the end it is impossible to ignore a baby elephant!

A mission statement should answer the following questions:

- Who are you?

- Who are your intended customers?

- What are your products or services?

- What qualities make you unique?

Without a mission statement, it is too easy to pursue single opportunities that lead away from long-term goals.

Competition via Mission Statement

Southwest Airlines has a one-sentence mission statement[14] that emphasizes warm and friendly customer service. It provides a model for focus and simplicity. Employees and customers can easily refer to its key phrases, including "highest quality of customer service". While their document does go on for a number of pages, it covers the mission statement in an extremely clear and concise manner.

Another instructive source is a compilation of Fortune 500 mission statements[15]. The American Standard company's statement is even more concise than the Southwest Airlines version. It lists customers, employees, and shareholders as its stakeholders.

---

[14] Southwest Airlines, "Mission Statement", revised May 17, 2012, at
http://www.southwest.com/assets/pdfs/corporate-commitments/customer-service-commitment.pdf .
[15] Mission Statements.com, "Fortune 500", at
http://www.missionstatements.com/fortune_500_mission_statements.html .

One of the most concise mission statements belongs to Auto-Owners' Insurance. In twelve words, it aspires to "provide the best claim service". Becton, Dickinson & Co. has an even shorter statement: "To help all people live healthy lives". At the other end of the spectrum, Avon Products requires a lengthy paragraph. It actually comprises six bullet points, each with a heading and a sentence. In general, the focus is on what the company will do and achieve, although it does mention its customers. Aflac's mission statement describes its strategy of "aggressive marketing", "quality products" and "competitive prices"; this is more "how to" than "mission and goal".

These mission statements show a variety of styles and goals. In my view, the best focus on serving the customer in a brief, concise manner. The worst simply list their current assets and practices. Such statements describe the present situation rather than providing aspirations and goals. Some of the statements seem to ignore business realities, such as the cost of "providing the best service" without noting cost control or efficiency.

A clear, concise, customer-focused mission statement is a powerful marketing tool. Add it to your web site's "About Us" page. Give it prominence in brochures and ads. Post a large-font copy in your office, store or factory to remind yourself, your employees, and your customers of your core mission.

Conserving and Pursuing Cash

Several issues are important for cash management in a careful and prudent small business.

Staying within the correct niche is an important part of conserving cash. Pursuing too many divergent opportunities will squander money by advertising too lightly in too many markets. It may require capital expenditures, procuring more raw materials, or hiring extra staff. In all cases, the two necessary steps are determining the policy and implementing the practice. Implementation takes ongoing effort and discipline across a variety of items.

Discretionary Spending

An obvious way to conserve cash is to minimize discretionary expenses. This section refers to current expenses, whether paid by cash, cheque, or credit card. The key is to avoid spending the company's money unnecessarily. Questions to ask include:

Page 69

- Will this purchase help to earn income?

- Will this purchase meet a business need, such as safety equipment or accounting records?

- Will this purchase help decrease other costs?

Timing the Payments

Payments should be made when required, but not sooner; and not later, so as to avoid late payment penalties.

Capital Expenditures

The strategy for capital investments is less obvious, so let's use an example. Suppose the business must deliver small products within an urban area. Several choices come to mind:

- Use a delivery service for each shipment to eliminate the capital investment but at a relatively high fixed cost per delivery.

- Lease a vehicle. The accounting entries show current expenses rather than an investment and payments are due monthly.

- Buy a vehicle, but use a loan. The bookkeeping accounts show a capital expenditure, monthly loan payments, and depreciation for the asset. This conserves most of the cash held as equity, but increases the liabilities.

- Buy a vehicle outright. This spends cash while minimizing monthly expenses, but still adds a depreciating asset to the books.

- Require the employee to provide her own vehicle; reimburse legitimate expenses but, again, avoid capital investment.

It is a straightforward task to construct a spreadsheet to evaluate these models for delivering products. Much of the work involves researching all the costs in each option. Insurance, fuel, licensing, maintenance, and repairs must be included in the operating costs for a vehicle.

Only the model of using a delivery service avoids incurring an employee's salary. In all other cases, the business has to pay someone to drive the vehicle! Both the delivery service and the employee-provided vehicle avoid capital expenditures.

The strategy cannot end simply by finding the least expensive solution that meets your current requirements. If your business grows, at what point would a different choice be more efficient? If there is a seasonal slump in demand, does the monthly operating cost remain the same? Could you deliver goods more quickly than the delivery service, and does that matter to your customers? Can you differentiate yourself from your competitors by offering a different delivery model? Or would your local circumstances make it advisable that you spin off a free-standing delivery service?

Accounts Receivable and the Pursuit of Cash

Few things are as frustrating in a small business as completing a sale without getting paid. Depending on the nature of the business, the possibilities include:

- Ensuring that terms of payment are clear at the start of a contract;

- Invoicing customers in a timely manner;

- Personally following up on delinquent accounts;

- Dedicating an employee to pursue receivables;

- Putting a lien on property or goods; and

- Selling receivables to a collection agency.

King David's Niche

The Old Testament records the Israelites' conquest of the land of Canaan from the time Joshua crossed the Jordan River, through the reigns of kings Saul and David several generations later. Later, from time to time, this territory was under attack, or even subdued, by foreign powers.

Yet even King David, for all his military success, did not seek to conquer the known world. The Israelites had enough difficulty achieving and maintaining their hold on the territory that had been promised to their ancestor Abraham. King David knew his niche and was content to work within it.

Summary for the Niche

The first strategy is to select and commit to a specific niche, based on current conditions and expected competitive advantage. The primary advantage for a small business owner is to apply local knowledge to your relationships to provide customized service or products.

The secondary advantage of working in a niche is that this can conserve cash by reducing early expenses for inventory and marketing.

Chapter 7 – STRATEGY #2: THE THREE PHASES OF CORPORATE TRANSFORMATION

Overview: Three Phases

Corporate Transformation is a three-step process that has been proven to work in a variety of businesses. Although it began as a last-ditch approach for large corporations as they faced collapse, the principles are successful for small companies as well. Nor is it required to wait until a business is failing! A healthy company has the luxury of implementing a later phase and still reaping a significant reward.

About half of all business ailments can be cured by making an accurate diagnosis because a clear statement of the problem points to its own solution.

Recognizing a Disaster in the Making

Typical warning signs of an unfolding business disaster include a declining position in your established markets and declining profitability (or a series of losses).

Corporate Transformation as a Remedy for an Ailing Business

The Corporate Transformation process uses the analogy of health care for a sick patient. The three phases are:

1.   Surgery: Drastic treatment, to stave off bankruptcy.

2.   Resuscitation: Waking up after surgery, to improve sales and profits.

3.   Nursing: Occupational therapy, to build the foundation for long-term sustainable growth.

Phase 1: Surgery: Saving the Business

Surgery is the most drastic type of medical treatment, but is appropriate for, say, a ruptured appendix. The diseased tissue is beyond repair and must be removed.

Business Problems That Require Surgery

A company may require "surgery" when it experiences severe problems, such as:

- Ongoing operating losses,

- Inability to make profitable changes, and/or

- Exhausted capital reserves.

A human illness may have internal or external causes. Influenza or a bullet wound results from external agents; whereas appendicitis, cancer, and obesity are caused internally.

Many companies experience problems through their own actions, inactions, or management style. By the medical analogy, these are "internal" ailments. The business owner might act hastily, throwing resources into ventures without due diligence. Or the management might vacillate, conducting so many studies that an opportunity is missed. Often the financial controls are weak, or there is little discipline for competitive sourcing. Low morale might be a cause – but is often a symptom – of a company in need of surgical treatment for flaws in its human resources management. If the operational costs are higher than the industry norm, the cause may lie with insufficient capital investment, weak operational management, or perhaps, weak financial controls or even embezzlement or fraud.

Internal problems may be divided into two categories. Let's use cancer as our analogy. A benign tumour is diseased tissue that has little effect outside of itself: it does not spread to other regions of the body. In a business, lazy or incompetent employees might form a benign tumour. They are not "healthy" and may cause morale problems for others.

By contrast, a malignant tumour actively spreads to other tissues and is likely to be fatal. Employees who actively undermine morale fit this category; even more so are those who break the law or fail to follow best practices when pursuing sales or profits.

The ailing business might blame increased competition, changes in government regulations, or a weakened economy for its current problems. These are external sources, outside the control of the business. The medical term for a cause of such a disease would be an "external virus". Yet an observer might ask, "What was your contingency plan? Do you not keep abreast of relevant industry news"?

Surgical Steps

Corporate surgical treatment generally consists of four main steps:

1.   Clear communication

2.   Concentrate on the core business

3.   Cost Control

4.   Cash Flow

Let us consider each step.

Clear Communication

In a large corporation, the CEO would appoint a core team to make and communicate the plans. The small business owner has far fewer people on staff, but must be clear in communicating both the new plans and the urgency with which results must be obtained. The CEO must not deliver ambiguous messages, but rather project a no-nonsense style of leadership. Naturally, in a small group, secrets are hard to keep; your employees have probably already seen the problems.

Concentrate on the Core Business

Concentrate on the basics. Conglomerates should sell off unprofitable divisions. What can the small business do? Perhaps, it is time to focus the marketing effort to promote only one product. Should you close the store but retain the online sales web site (or vice versa)? Certainly it is time to put the expansion plans on hold.

Control Costs

Reduce debt by selling unused or underutilized assets. The key is to break even or turn a profit as quickly as possible without closing the business altogether.

Is it possible or feasible to control costs by downsizing the staff? Would they accept reduced or deferred wages instead? Would it be better to sell the delivery van and use a courier, or lease a van rather than pay the courier fees? The general rule is to evaluate both the position and the employee. Since there had been some reason for creating and staffing the position in the first place, the most logical starting point is to motivate employees to put forth their best efforts.

When downsizing, explore alternatives to actually dismissing employees. Would they accept reduced pay or benefits as an alternative to losing their jobs? Would they accept working on a part-time basis rather than seeing some of their co-workers terminated? Could management offer incentives based on future profitability? If the long-term plan requires today's staffing levels, there is little point in permanently losing good employees. Remember that successful companies perform above the average of their peers by consistently innovating in productive ways. They do not have high employee turnover.

Cash Flow

Cash flow is improved by invoicing and then collecting receivables promptly, and by stretching payments to the limit negotiated with suppliers. One common weak area is accounts receivable. Establish and clearly communicate, in writing, reasonable credit terms for your customers. Pursue overdue accounts by telephone, in person, or through legal action if required. Remember to qualify your new customer leads. Run a credit check before contracting to supply goods that might never be reimbursed.

Phase 2: Resuscitation: The Pursuit of Profitability

After surgery, the first task is to resuscitate the patient; to bring her back to consciousness.

Resuscitating a Small Business

The task for this phase is to improve sales volume and profit margins. As Mehrdad Baghai said, "Successful companies must grow new businesses. That is what leads to sustained profitable growth".

The first emphasis is on marketing and sales promotions. Start with a low-cost promotion; perhaps simply a new slogan for an existing product or service. This provides a reason for the sales force to make direct contact with existing customers and new prospects. If the business owner is also the whole sales staff, she must schedule herself to make these contacts. Include the slogan when advertising through various media.

Note that it is inappropriate to drive sales volume strictly by reducing prices. While this can increase sales, it erodes the profit margin. If the company has just had surgery, it probably cannot afford to "work for free". Instead, find other ways to increase sales.

The Internet is an awesome, low-cost advertising medium, although it can be an absolute failure if approached poorly. It takes planning, just like any marketing campaign. To use social media effectively requires a dedicated resource to initiate and maintain contact with every respondent. Planning, designing, and building a website require professional attention for measurable and timely results.

Profit margins should increase mainly because non-core and unprofitable product segments were amputated during "Surgery". Nonetheless, it is vital to control costs and monitor results. "A/B testing" should reveal whether campaign "A" or "B" actually converts more prospects into paying customers.

Profit margins depend on pricing; but lower prices should deliver a higher volume of sales in a price-conscious market. Therefore, two important strategic questions are "Who are my customers?" and "What does my brand represent?" Are your customers willing to pay a premium for quality or do they look for the cheapest product that works well enough? Does your pricing reflect what your customers expect? Answering these questions will help inform your decisions on pricing.

Sometimes, the pricing decisions themselves determine the apparent quality of a brand. One retailer in rural Indonesia sells hand-stitched quilts on a commission basis. If a particular quilt did not sell at its first price, the price was raised so new customers would perceive it as more valuable, and therefore, worth purchasing.

Marketing and Advertising for Resuscitation

Marketing and advertising are vital to increase sales. If you have used traditional media for advertising, you are aware of the expense involved in newspaper, radio, and television advertising. Once you are confident of your product, consider using the Internet to expand your advertising within a limited budget. However, it is vital to plan the marketing strategy before starting such a campaign.

If you need this advice, then you also need to contract a seasoned and successful Internet marketing specialist. The conversion page must lead to a measurable action, such as contacting your company or making an online purchase. Each landing page must address the specific issue that led your prospect to it and also clearly lead to the call to action. Both your online advertising and company blog must use the key phrases that customers seek when they consider buying your class of products. Finally, social relationship media provide a sense of personal contact for prospects and customers.

The components of an integrated online marketing campaign do have costs. You need to invest time in planning, while you also spend money for the professional marketing service. However, it is both possible and highly advantageous to set a budget ahead of time. Besides avoiding unforeseen expenses, this forces the Internet marketing professional to examine options and focus on the core message.

Another advantage of Internet marketing is that it should, and can, be designed to provide valuable information. These campaigns can deliver performance statistics such as the number of visitors per day, the number of desired actions that result (to contact or purchase), and the monetary value of these actions. Advertising campaigns should limit the daily expenditure so costs do not mount without review. Finally, perform "A/B" tests to determine which advertising copy actually delivers more customers.

Phase 3: Nursing: Occupational Therapy to Re-Train the Business

Depending on the surgical procedure, the patient may need therapy to regain strength and mobility, or to make adjustments after a limb is amputated.

Long-Term Nursing Tasks for a Small Business

At this point, the business is not in immediate danger of failure. Cash flow, sales, and profit margins have improved. One might think it would all be clear sailing. Not so. The major challenge is to maintain profitable growth after these critical one-time successes. The next tasks are:

- To identify the lessons learned from the first two phases and

- To apply that knowledge by changing the mind-set within the business.

Why was your business in trouble – so much trouble that it required surgery and resuscitation?

Sometimes the answer is simple. Perhaps lax accounting allowed costs to escalate or receivables to go uncollected. Rigid adherence to one process might have stifled innovation or flexibility, leading to missed sales or dissatisfied customers. Conversely, too much flexibility may have led to longer processing times and missed deadlines, or to accepting custom work with no profit margins. Often a combination of reasons caused the business crisis.

However many causes of the problems, these must be addressed as a condition for the long-term success of your business. For a large enterprise, this requires a change in the corporate culture. Large organizations take on a "personality". Initially, the mind-set is based on the CEO or founder. Later, it permeates the entire company, resisting change even upon changes of ownership or leadership.

Small companies reflect even more closely the personal qualities of the owner or manager. How then can a small business change? Clearly, the change starts with the owner or manager.

The Primary Task in Phase Three: to Embrace Change

The primary task may be the most difficult: to embrace the need for change and to actively seek change. In a large conglomerate, this begins with the CEO and board of directors, moving down through the hierarchy to the rank and file. These changes often include an increased focus on satisfying customer needs, greater teamwork with less office politics, ongoing training and improvement of efficiency and effectiveness, and pursuit of profitable innovation rather than maintenance of the status quo.

When a large enterprise follows the path of corporate transformation, it is too easy for employees to lose sight of the need for continuous improvement. It is important for the company to periodically remind itself of this cornerstone corporate philosophy to ensure that there is no substantial deviation or omission along its corporate journey. A sole proprietor or the staff of a small business might be more mindful, but reminders are helpful nonetheless.

A small business has fewer layers of employees, but similar goals. The owner and manager must seek change:

- Ask questions in every area of the business. Let's use marketing as an example.

    o How do we advertise currently? (Print, radio, TV, Internet).

    o What are we not doing yet? (Social media marketing; billboards).

    o What is our message? (Value; quality; convenience).

    o What new message should we promote? (Service; solution to a problem).

- Plan for the changes. We continue with the marketing example.

    o Add a coupon to the print advertisements because we do not know how many customers are being influenced by this medium. Pick a loss leader product, set a budget, and develop a way to track coupon redemptions.

    o Add a social marketing approach to our existing Internet presence. Plan to emphasize "reliable service" with a message about the low rate of returns or complaints. Budget for a short-term consultant and a new employee whose primary role is to be the "voice" of the online social medium.

- Take action to make these changes happen.

It's important to realize that this is not a one-time project; it is an attitude and a behaviour that initiates a series of projects.

The ability to recognize desirable changes may be limited by a person's education or experience, so further learning is essential. Often this learning experience requires taking courses, attending seminars, reading books, or networking with peers.

To lead a successful turnaround through all its phases, the CEO must have a specific mind-set. In the Nursing stage, this must be shared and fostered throughout the organization. The mind-set includes the willingness to embrace change, the courage to try new things, and the acceptance of interim failures while pursuing worthwhile goals.

Long-term success comes by achieving the correct business culture. This requires addressing the "heart" and not just using the "head". People will follow their hearts – their emotions, their ethics, their dreams and desires – far more readily and "wholeheartedly" than their heads. Yes, do communicate the logic and specific tasks. But share and nurture the vision for what your small business should become. When people buy into the vision and put their hearts into their work, success will follow.

Specific Tactics in the Nursing Stage: Globalization, Tribal Marketing, Word of Mouth, and Social Media

The Internet makes it possible for any small business to advertise and compete in the global market and also to focus on its own neighbourhood. Although globalization imposes a serious threat to any localized small business, the "Nursing Therapy" phase is the time to consider a counter-strike:

- Develop a web site to advertise your product or service.

- Search for low-cost but reliable suppliers…based anywhere in the world.

- After researching the shipping costs, consider advertising to everyone in the world.

"Tribal Marketing" refers to developing a community that will pass your advertising message for you through "Word of Mouth". Facebook's portfolio of games is a fine example. By its nature, Facebook aggregates communities of "friends," people who share some common interest or relationship. Facebook wants people to stay on their site as long as possible, so it promotes on-site games and encourages its users to share their achievements with their friends. Repeated exposure to these messages often leads to more people signing up for games. Thus, tribal marketing is simply advertising to a specific group of people who share some common features. As consumers promote the product to their acquaintances, it becomes a word of mouth campaign.

The underlying tool making these approaches possible is the use of social media. At the least, both computer-based Internet media and mobile cell-phone technologies allow people to remain in contact with others over extended periods of time. Any business can and should build a presence in at least one social media space and dedicate resources to expanding into new positions as time and budget permit.

This does require dedication and investment. One advantage over traditional media is the relative ease of measuring the effectiveness of a campaign. Perhaps the only equivalent in print media is the use of printed coupons, tagged with the source. Then one can tally all the coupons redeemed from newspaper A versus flyer B after the campaign closes to determine how many shoppers actually used these coupons, and from which source. Web-based promotions, by contrast, can be developed to provide such statistics at a more detailed level and without the need to store and count the redemptions.

Jonathan, Saul's Son and David's Friend

At one time, King Saul's son Jonathan had begun a battle that went well for Israel, because the Philistines began fighting each other. Saul then led the main group of soldiers, but swore an oath that no one could eat anything until the victory had been secured. Since Jonathan had been isolated in his own vanguard, he did not learn of this unusual order. As the day wore on, the Israelite soldiers grew famished. Jonathon ate some wild honey that he found in a wooded area, but no one else had any. As it turned out, it would have been wiser for Saul to permit his troops to eat: for the soldiers' physical strength, for their religious integrity, and for their morale[16]. Thus it is very important to administer the right medicine and know which stage or combination of stages that the company is experiencing; otherwise, there is no efficacy in the implementation.

Summary for Three-Stage Business Transformation

When a small business or a large corporation is critically ill, a three-step business transformation process can restore it to health. The phases correspond to hospital treatment: surgery to stem the bleeding (of cash); resuscitation to bring the patient to consciousness (and increased sales); and long-term nursing therapy (to train the organization to make ongoing changes for healthy profits). A company that is not

---

[16] I Samuel 14, particularly from verses 23-30.

on the brink of disaster might also benefit by applying the second or third stages of the transformation process.

Chapter 8 – STRATEGY #3: PRODUCTIVE INNOVATION AND INNOVATIVE PRODUCTIVITY

Sometimes "innovation" is the slave of productivity: the only research a company performs is aimed at increasing the efficiency of existing processes. Other companies spend all their time in an effort to develop new products, but never achieve efficient manufacturing and marketing techniques. Too often, either productivity comes at the expense of innovation, or the pursuit of innovation drives out productivity. There is too little investment of time or money in a balanced approach to innovation and productivity.

The key to success in business is to pursue both.

The only serious danger for an innovative company lies in continuing to invest in a dying market. To rephrase an old adage, "A falling tide strands all ships". There is no point in making a better Betamax video recording system or in making more at lower unit prices: they had already been replaced by VHS, which itself has been supplanted by digital technologies. Profits follow productivity only if the market for the product remains strong.

By contrast, a company's competitors may introduce a new service that renders the current offerings obsolete. At that time, it may be too late to become innovative. "The best defence is a good offence", and it is better to continually innovate than to await defeat by a creative competitor.

The Example of the American Rust Belt

Several states in the USA had been known as the "steel belt". Large steel mills supplied Detroit with sheet metal for the automobile industry. These large companies invested to become highly productive for large batches of standard-grade steel at ever lower costs. Their other customers included manufacturers of large household appliances, such as refrigerators, washers and dryers, and other durable goods.

Over time, as these various customers developed their products, they began to demand different chemistries and characteristics for the steel. Each coil of steel was ordered with specific requirements, such as tensile or ductile strength, rust resistance, and a host of other features.

As well, it became economically feasible to recycle iron or steel from scrap yards as part of the feedstock for a mill, in addition to pure iron as refined from mines. At the same time, Japanese and other foreign manufacturers took market share away from the domestic steel mills.

The result was a proliferation of "mini-mills". They invested in newer equipment that could switch the chemistry from one batch to the next. These mini-mills were profitable with smaller production runs than the hulking legacy steel mills, which had relinquished the capability to innovate in the pursuit of capacity and productivity. The older, larger, less innovative and, in some cases, defunct steel mills characterize the American "rust belt".

Definitions of Productivity and Innovation

One cannot achieve what remains undefined. Without a description of the destination, how can one know when it has been reached?

Definitions of Productivity

Productivity is the "result" divided by the "effort", or the "output" divided by the "input". Productivity can take many forms:

- Labour productivity = production per unit of time

  - The number of items produced per hour, per shift, per year

  - The weight, area or volume of material processed per hour

  - Similar productivity measures may apply to manufacturing machinery, as well as industrial processes

- Financial productivity = revenue divided by expense

- This metric might be calculated within categories:

  - Labour productivity = production per dollar for direct labour

  - Sales productivity = revenue per dollar of commission

  - Advertising productivity = revenue per advertising dollar

  - Investment productivity = revenue per dollar of capital investment

- These metrics might also be calculated for incremental expenses:

  - Increased revenue for every extra dollar spent on advertising or capital investment

- Sales productivity = revenue per sales call

  - Another sales productivity measure = percentage of deals made per sales call

  - Yet another sales productivity measure = number of deals made per hour or week

- Marketing productivity = number of responses for a given campaign

  - Advertising productivity = number of responses divided by the cost of the campaign

  - Advertising productivity = number of responses divided by the number of ad impressions

- Call centre productivity = number of inquiries or service requests completed per hour

In many situations, productivity should distinguish gross versus net production. It may be important to manufacture 200 widgets per hour at a peak rate, but how many are free of defects? Perhaps the process can only produce 180 defect-free widgets per hour, taking preventative maintenance and quality control into account. Similarly, a "fast talking" sales presentation might generate more revenue per hour, but suffer a higher cancellation rate when the customers review their options and have second thoughts.

A Classic Productivity Trap

One of the classic problems with measuring productivity is caused by choosing the wrong metric. The problem often arises when measuring productivity, where an unwise choice of metrics may give poor direction to employees. Manufacturing more goods, but with a higher defect rate, may result in fewer acceptable products to ship to customers, or in higher returns, with even higher costs to correct the problems. It is easy to count the number of widgets produced during a shift; it takes longer, but can be more important, to determine the defect rate and include "number of acceptable widgets" and "cost per acceptable widget" in the daily production report.

Consider a call centre that rewards the staff by the number of calls answered per hour. An unscrupulous employee might give useless advice, simply to end the conversation in the shortest time. A better metric must include checking on the customer's satisfaction with the advice. This might be automated by assuming that a second call from the same telephone number indicates dissatisfaction, although that might not be true either.

Another example arises when sales commissions skew sales in an undesired direction. Consider a sales person who is likely to promote the product that offers her the largest commission. If the company's goal is actually to promote a different product, the results will not be optimal. Worse, the commission might override the seller's instinct to suggest the product most suited to her customer's need. Even if this meets the company's short-term goal, it might harm customer retention and repeat business.

Resources for Productivity

A small business with a small staff may find that the employees themselves are the greatest untapped resource for productivity. These people perform the work on a daily basis and often have excellent ideas for doing things in easier ways. The manager's challenge then is to motivate and reward productivity improvements while maintaining quality and adherence to regulatory requirements. The employees may not know why they have to maintain detailed records or clean the equipment. Yet they may devise better ways to make those records or do the cleaning.

Sometimes it is necessary to enlist an outside consultant. A manufacturing company might need to help starting a kanban or 5S system. Perhaps an IT consultant can recommend software to integrate sales with accounting and manufacturing.

Another important question for productivity is, "Does this task add value"? For example, should you discontinue the advertising channel that produced the fewest sales in the past year?

One trap some manufacturers encounter is sending an order slip with the work-in-process. Suppose the order had specified a custom fastener that is not in stock. Simply delaying the shipment without explanation will annoy the customer. Should the foreman be empowered to change the order in order to meet the delivery schedule? Will this change be considered a defect when the customer inspects the finished product? Would it not be wiser to require customer authorization before making changes?

The Importance of Measuring Productivity

As famed IT consultant Tom DeMarco said in *Controlling Software Projects: Management, Measurement and Estimation*, "You can't control what you can't measure".

So true! In the first place, a manager or owner has no control over what has not been measured: there is no true knowledge of the situation without a measurement. Second, employees will focus their attention on the tasks or issues that are measured. The squeaky wheel gets the grease and so the measured activity will be performed.

In general, productivity is measured as "output divided by input". Manufacturing examples include the number of widgets assembled per hour, the number of widgets per employee, or the wholesale value of widgets divided by the cost of materials and labour. Sometimes other metrics are required, such as the number of widgets divided by energy consumption (such as electricity or natural gas). Some processes, such as firing clay pots in a kiln, are more energy efficient if the unit is filled; it takes energy to heat the kiln itself. Other manufacturing processes use the same energy for each unit being produced.

In the financial realm, return on equity or return on investment are common productivity measurements. Another is profitability as the total operating profit divided by the percentage of inventory turned over during that period. Less well known are: Dividend Covers, the current year's profits divided by the dividends paid to shareholders, and the Gearing Ratio, which is the percentage of debt divided by the total of debt plus equity.

Marketing may measure the number of responses or sales, divided by the cost of the campaign. Internet sites log the number of visits and views per day[17]; the percentage of "clicks" on advertisements per thousand visitors; the rate of conversion from visitor to contact or customer; visits, views, or conversions per day; and many other numbers that determine visitor engagement with the site.

Sales performance metrics include the number of contracts closed per hundred sales calls, the total revenue divided by the number of salespersons, or the revenue divided by salary in the sales department.

Reducing the number of defects, or the amount of waste, are other ways to improve productivity. Although the quality metric is usually the error percentage, that is simply the inverse of the productivity metric for success: the percentage of acceptable products created by the process during the measurement period. The same is applied to reducing waste.

Another inverted productivity measure is the cost per widget; this is simply the inverse of widgets/dollar.

DeMarco had made the point that IT projects in particular suffer from unreliable estimates and, therefore, cost overruns, missed deadlines, and low satisfaction for upper management. He proposed measuring the quality of these estimates and introduced a discipline to review IT projects much as one would review a manufacturing process. A particular machine should produce N widgets per hour, taking maintenance and other down time into consideration. If that machine cannot do so, either it is defective or there are other problems in the manufacturing process. Likewise, if a one-time project does not deliver its results on time and within budget, either the project was under-estimated or the rest of the project methodology is flawed. Just as one repairs a defective machine, so one ought to correct the project methodology.

One often neglected way to increase manufacturing productivity is to reduce the defect ratio. The productivity metric is "acceptable products divided by all products manufactured". If you make 90 acceptable widgets out of 100, you wasted the labour and raw materials for 10 of those widgets. Increase the quality to 95%, and productivity automatically increased. The Six Sigma discipline, while

---

[17] The number of *visits* indicates how many people went to the site, regardless of whether they viewed one page or many. The number of *views* relates to the number of pages viewed. One visitor might view three pages; or three visitors each looked at only one page.

generally associated with major corporations, can be adapted to systematically reducing the defect rate in almost any process for almost any endeavour.

A Definition for Innovation

In a narrow sense, an innovation is something "new" that has been developed. Innovative methods are new ways of doing things. Implicitly, innovations are improvements, not just novelties. In the context of a competitive business, innovation cannot simply be "new", or even better. The innovation must also be effective and profitable; it must have a positive impact on the business. Thus innovation is defined as a good idea that gets successfully implemented, utilized or commercialized. Otherwise, innovation is just another passing idea.

Pure science is sometimes criticized for failing to deliver viable products, at least at the time of the invention or discovery. By 1875, the Crookes tube could generate X-rays. It took over twenty-five years before this was applied commercially. Today, every month sees a list of research papers breathlessly explaining that yet another tiny step has been taken toward quantum computing. Someday, this may lead to a thriving business in computing. At the moment, the equipment usually must be refrigerated in liquid helium and cannot yet store one character or count to one hundred.

A commercial innovation, therefore, is a new, practical product or method than can be implemented "quickly" and profitably.

How Productivity and Innovation Interact

Ideally, one maintains a careful balance between productivity and innovation. An important priority for time and task management is to schedule and budget the ongoing pursuit of each goal.

Wisely managed, productivity and innovation complement one another. Moore's Law states the prediction that the "number of transistors built into a computer chip" will double every eighteen months. That time period partly reflects the effort to innovate the new chips, and particularly, the innovative engineering required to achieve the next level of miniaturization. It also reflects the time required to make and sell enough of the new generation of chips to pay for the next round of innovation. Companies such as Intel balance their productivity and their innovative resources to

Page 90

profitably foster new products. IBM and Trek Technology joined forces to bring the first USB drives to the consumer market in 2000; later improvements in productivity have reduced the price for these popular PC storage units.

Poor resource management, or poor focus, can allow these tasks to compete with each other. Singapore and many other countries are placing their future in innovation and productivity to boost its economic growth. However, what Singapore needs most is not increasing productivity or innovation alone. Improving productivity innovatively and innovating productively shall be the key thrust for our economy.

What Drives Business Innovation?

Both science and consumer tastes change rapidly. Innovation cannot be driven by reviewing the latest technology, regardless of whether it was introduced by your competitors or developed in-house. Neither can recent or historic trends predict what will be trendy or desirable in the future.

That is not to say that such research is completely wasted. One may certainly learn a lot from past and current successes and failures.

Yet the best starting point for innovation is what the current market demands from popular suppliers. This provides a good target for innovation: something at the edge of one's capabilities that also has a demonstrated market.

One long-running trend worthy of examination is pre-recorded music. During the record-player era, long-play albums (LPs) packaged a group of songs as selected by the production company. A less expensive alternative was the "single" which held only two songs. Price and convenience were drivers for some purchasing decisions, but a record player was a desktop device rather than a portable one. Later, cassette tape recorders allowed consumers to produce their own sequences of songs from a variety of sources and also made that music portable. MP3 players and other solid-state devices have continued the trend toward personalized and portable music. Presumably, any new innovation that provides greater portability or customization of a music collection could become popular.

In any service industry, customer feedback is the key to successful implementation of an innovation. Such feedback is easier for a small business to obtain. As noted earlier, the decision maker is quite close to the customers.

Remember that your existing customers return because they appreciate the service they have been receiving. A change might be unsettling, so explain any change and solicit the customer's opinion. A formal checklist or rating sheet helps focus the feedback, but be sure to allow a paragraph "in your own words".

If the innovation is a result of previously obtained customer opinion, then it is more likely to be accepted by at least some of your clientele. Be sure to check with those who provided their opinions in the first place, to determine whether you succeeded in pleasing them.

Consider whether this innovation is an expansion of your service offering, or a change to an existing service. Some customers may stop buying if they dislike the change. Can you afford to lose them, or were they an unprofitable drain on your resources?

Finally, advertise the innovation and the opportunity for providing feedback. This may lead to new customers. Internet marketing campaigns can be shaped around new offerings and the social engagement that comes with offering opinions.

One service provider with an interesting track record for innovation is Facebook. It is wildly popular and continues to grow its user base as an Internet social platform. Facebook periodically rolls out innovations in the services and in the way the services are presented to the users. Every innovation is greeted with informal feedback from vocal users: "Facebook changed <whatever>. How can I change it back? Why did they change it"?

Both Facebook, founded by Mark Zuckerberg, and Twitter, founded by Jack Dorsey, Biz Stone and others, are social network platforms with the intrinsic capability to share brief messages among users. When these messages contain complaints about poor service from a well-known supplier, the message can "go viral" by being shared and passed along again and again. Larger companies should monitor these social media streams to learn of problems and deal with them before they generate too much bad publicity. A small business can plan and execute a marketing or feedback strategy using these same tools: advertise the innovation, request feedback, and respond to what is said.

The duel between social platforms Myspace and Facebook is an instructive example of competition through innovation. Myspace had the earlier success, having based its first features on the popular earlier Friendster gaming and social networking platform. It then emphasized the entertainment industry, primarily popular music.

Myspace also decided to develop its applications in-house. Facebook built a platform for which outside developers could construct apps. Zynga's provision of its games inside Facebook is a sterling example of how successful this can be. Playing games keeps users logged into the main site, where they can continue to interact socially. As well, the social platform can promote the games as a way for people to "meet" and interact.

Perhaps the greatest problem for Myspace was that it seemed more vulnerable to user misconduct than Facebook. Whether or not the comparisons were valid, the perception took hold that Myspace had more "spam" announcements, weaker privacy, and other problems than Facebook.

At least one useful Myspace innovation became a problem. Many sites, such as Facebook, do not allow their users to tweak or adjust the layout or appearance of the page. Myspace, by contrast, permitted users to enter HTML and CSS codes to alter their personal profile pages. Since making an effort leads to a greater sense of commitment, this was a good idea to retain users. However, it takes some skill and practice to do a good job with these coding tools. A safer practice is to give users a set of simplified controls to change very specific cosmetic features, such as a profile photograph.

In the world of computer technology, it takes strong project management skills to achieve the intended value from a project. All social network companies must spend significant amounts annually to build and maintain an innovative and secure site. In addition, such sites must function well and reliably, and be easily mastered by new users. Myspace sometimes reported an annual loss because their revenues declined while costs for technical staff remained.

A web site to promote a business does not need nearly so much effort or expense, although it is worthwhile to pay a skilled professional to design an e-commerce site where purchases are made. The small business owner should focus on a simple, clean design; a clear message; and a schedule of regular updates for the business site.

The general lesson for competitive innovation by any small business is to continue innovating even when enjoying success. That very success will attract competitors who might analyze your current practices and develop novel services, products, or ways to deliver them.

The Perils of Efficiency without Innovation

A company with a single focus on productivity will deliberately avoid innovation, except possibly in pursuit of efficiency. Such a business might make a profit in the short term. However, it will be left behind when a nimble competitor introduces an innovative product. Memorex began by selling tape reels for IBM mainframe computers, and later competed with IBM in making storage devices for those same computers. For several decades, Memorex was efficient and profitably sold these products at a lower cost. After being sold to Burroughs, a rival of IBM, this aspect of Memorex's product line was passed from corporation to corporation. While the brand name lingers, Memorex never could innovate products that moved beyond the edge of what other companies had already created.

An earlier example is the classic American steel industry, with a focus on economies of scale and productivity improvements. The pursuit of efficiency through sales volume and size of infrastructure led to the inability to create innovative products for emerging niche markets. And let's remember that those "niche markets" resulted from the innovations created by their long-term customers in the manufacturing sector.

Innovation without Productivity is Innovation without Profit

Some companies innovate but fail to turn a profit on their invention or improvement. While these failures may be caused by insufficient development, timid marketing, or some other flaw in implementation, the main reason for missing the benefits of a breakthrough is the failure to implement the innovation productively.

Companies that remain innovative but neglect productivity cannot increase in efficiency. They may never begin to realize a profit. At some time, one must be satisfied with the existing product but focus, for a time, on improving the profit margin.

Another view of "productivity" is to determine whether the innovation improves sales volumes. In the short term, test changes in pricing or marketing strategies. If you produce and market a "family of products", what happens if you change the mixture?

Focus on results by measuring your success after setting objectives for your sales against your competitors.

An industry with a long history of successfully marrying productivity to innovation is personal computing. One joke says it well: if automobiles rivalled personal computers for innovation and productivity breakthroughs, we would be driving cars that cost a dollar, cruise at hundreds of miles per hour while burning only one gallon of gasoline per thousand miles; but the car would be the size of a postage stamp.

Productive Innovation and Innovative Productivity

Three key questions to consider during the innovation process are:

- Is the market (almost) ready for this innovation?

    o If we need to persuade customers that they need it...perhaps they won't buy it.

    o If we need to persuade customers that they need it...perhaps the marketing campaign will take too long and be too costly.

    o Is the innovation minor enough that customers will switch gladly?

- Will this innovation be commercially viable?

    o What price could this product command among current or future customers?

    o Can we manufacture and ship this product profitably at that price?

- Can and will we market this innovation?

    o Are we experienced in marketing this type of product?

    o Do we have the resources to plan and execute the advertising campaign?

Earlier we had noted that television talent shows had revived an older concept. The new version included an innovation that had not been available in the previous generation: viewer participation through voting via telephone, text messages, or Internet web sites. The television producers did not develop those technical innovations. Rather, they recognized and exploited technology that had appeared and was being used by others. The cost for this technology was small by the standards of a television show, and no doubt was defrayed by charging for the phone and text message vote processes.

Yet, this innovative technology was also very productive. So long as the call centre or web server was able to handle the volume of votes, keeping track of the voting had no particular labour costs. In addition, once the basic format for the talent competition was developed in one country, it was exported to other markets around the world. The "Idol", "…Got Talent", and "…Dance" formats varied the details, but each used similar technologies and could be transferred to different nations with relatively little effort beyond recruiting the judges and hosts.

Once your company has made an innovation that gains acceptance in the market, the new questions should focus on productivity, including profit margins:

- How can we improve our productivity:

    o Manufacturing: How to simplify and standardize the manufacturing process?

    o Purchasing: Order larger quantities for a discount?

    o Marketing: Use customer testimonials or social marketing to improve our advertising efficiency?

    o Sales: Train the employees to improve the manufacturing or sales processes?

- Can we improve the profit margin through pricing?

    o Are the customers committed to the product for its features or benefits?

        ▪ If so, can we raise prices without losing too many sales?

    o Are customers very sensitive to price?

        ▪ If so, would a price reduction lead to increased sales?

- Would the increased sales lead to volume efficiencies, thereby improving the profit margin?

Can Innovation Be Measured?

Productivity metrics have already been discussed. Perhaps it comes as a surprise that corporate innovation can also be measured. We can measure the innovation in terms of the propensity of the company to introduce and implement innovative initiatives. We can measure the innovation culture through the corporate policies, strategies and tactics of the company to implement innovation. Quite often, companies are not short of innovative ideas but it is the implementation that goes wrong or does not get kick-off.

Consider an employee suggestion programme, which can be started with the classic "suggestion box" to hold submissions written on paper. A typical process involves reviewing each suggestion; determining whether to discard it or try it upon first reading; trying out the suggestion; and then accepting, modifying, or rejecting the suggestion after a trial.

One obvious metric is Annual Gross Innovations (AGI) per employee: how many suggestions does each employee make, on average, during a year? Another is Annual Implemented Innovations (AII) per employee, or the number of accepted suggestions per employee per year.

Financial metrics include the cost of the suggestion programme, as well as the net savings or net increased revenues per employee or per suggestion. The budget should target the overall expenditures, and track the improvements due to implementing the suggestions.

The best suggestion programmes reward employees, especially with a percentage of the incremental savings or revenue, for a specific time period after the suggestion is implemented. Non-monetary recognition might also be given, but remember that employees who feel poorly rewarded are unlikely to develop their second innovation.

In fact, one useful management innovation is the Staff Satisfaction Index, or SSI, which measures the employees' engagement with corporate innovation goals and satisfaction with the company. A major corporation might hire a consulting firm to administer and evaluate the index, to ensure that employees are not penalized for expressing unfavourable opinions about their managers. The owner of a very small company might simply take note of the effort and enthusiasm exhibited by each employee, especially with respect to situations such as a customer complaint delivered just before closing time. When adopting an SSI measurement process, include a section on employee participation in pursuit of productive innovation.

How to Foster Productive Innovation

Several criteria must be met to foster and nourish a climate of productive innovation. The pursuit of innovation is a competitive advantage simply because most companies fail to do it well.

Three Requirements to Foster Productive Innovation

First, management must state their desire for innovation and follow up by allocating resources. The process does not require huge cash flow from profits or new capital from investors, but it does require some investment. The main resource is time. Form a team with the mandate to pursue innovation as part of the workday. Allot a budget for some materials, which might include new tools or equipment; but it might be possible to partner with government or educational institutions and use their facilities for specific tests.

Second, it is important not to punish those who make the attempt but fail to deliver a successful innovation. Thomas Edison said, "It was not a thousand failures, but rather a thousand steps to the right solution". Learn from the experience and consider how to do better the next time. A salesperson does not close every deal. Innovators are likely to have a lower "batting average" when exploring the unknown than an experienced person selling a good product to interested clientele. Don't punish the innovator or despair of innovating; simply keep seeking ways to improve the process.

Third, management must set and enforce the rules for successful innovation. The goal is to have a marketable product that can be sold profitably. One approach is to set a budget for each project, with the requirement of a formal application and approved process. On the other hand, Google automatically budgets "Innovation Time Off" for employees to work on their own projects. Each company will find its own balance of supervision and flexibility. This may change over time, as the operation grows or evolves.

Companies achieve maturity in innovation by establishing processes to nurture new ideas. One example comes from the discipline of project management. No project is complete without producing a review document discussing the successes and "areas for improvement" for the project leadership process.

Process innovation is often sparked by "bottleneck busters": the people who recognize issues in work flow and are willing to overcome the problems. Sometimes the solution is a technological gadget, such as a pencil sharpener or photocopier to overcome clerical delays. More often, however, a "bottleneck buster" improves efficiency by asking "Why" or "Why not..."? One example is to empower a secretary to purchase standard office supplies, within a specific budget, as the need arises. This can save the time and effort required to complete requisition forms and obtain signatures. Other process innovations shift workflow to the most appropriate employees: whether a receptionist or the service-providing professional should take standard notes at the start of an interview depends on their relative pay scales, plus the importance of using that interview to build rapport and perhaps probe more deeply depending on the initial answers.

Recognize that different people have different skills. Some will be better at making incremental improvements to productivity. They will tweak and adjust to squeeze better performance out of a business process or a machine. Other people have the imagination and courage to eliminate a time-wasting procedure or to automate a quality control step. Both types make valuable contributions, if appropriately guided and rewarded. The key is how to transform the organisation to take care of the productivity and innovation. We will call the combination of productivity and innovation measurements as Corporate Transformation Index.

Thus, Productivity and Innovation depend on effective and efficient corporate transformation or improving efficiency effectively and effectiveness efficiently

> Corporate Transformation Index^{TM}
> = Productivity @ Innovation
> = Output/Input x Innovation Culture

Biology provides some instructive examples of success or failure in the light of productivity or innovation.

The dinosaurs were extremely successful for millions of years, but the word now describes an institution that has outlived its usefulness and is failing to adapt to changing circumstances. A recent view is that the dinosaurs had become similar to modern business conglomerates: they filled every ecological niche as they grew from small hatchlings to giants. The problem was that the whole species was vulnerable if any niche collapsed. Hypothetically, a young herbivore might depend on smaller plants that might recover quickly after a forest fire. Conversely, the adult herbivore might graze only on the tallest and largest plants. If those plants died out in that same forest fire, it might take years before the next generation grew large enough for the adult dinosaurs to eat. By then, the adults would have starved; therefore no juveniles would have been born, and the population would become extinct – which is what happened. A current theory[18] is that modern birds are dinosaurs that reach sexual maturity while still very small. They only occupy ecological niches appropriate to their small size, so they are relatively immune to some disasters.

For the business analogy, the dinosaur would be a conglomerate that mines and refines ore into metal, designs and builds the car from that metal, drills and refines petroleum as fuel for the car, builds roads, licenses drivers, and sells insurance. It's a wonderful monopoly until someone invents ultra-light carbon-fibre solar-powered personal aircraft.

On the other hand, the cockroach has outlasted the dinosaur. As a small but quick insect, the cockroach is not a picky eater. It scurries out of sight before most people can squash it and it reproduces in vast numbers. Any one cockroach might share a "niche" with many relatives: behind a baseboard in the kitchen, for example.

Small businesses can flourish by remaining small, nimble, and ready to exploit every small opportunity.

---

[18] Bhart-Anjan Bhullar and Arkhat Abzhanov (University of Texas at Austin), as reported in "*Birds Evolved From Dinosaurs By Remaining 'Juveniles'*", IB Times. (May 31, 2012). http://www.ibtimes.co.uk/articles/20120531/birds-evolved-from-dinosaurs-remaining-039-juveniles-039.htm

To Summarize Innovation and Productivity

Increasing a company's productivity is a recognized tactic in business competition; it permits sales at lower prices or creates larger profits.

Unfortunately, the pursuit of productivity is like an endless military campaign, with many costly but indecisive battles. Yet neither side can afford to lose the warm so the war continues.

In *The Art of War*, Sun Tze noted that a country cannot afford protracted wars. The peasants cannot continue to supply food, nor can the artisans manufacture arms, for an extended campaign. His solution was to win decisively and quickly, using superior tactics based on military intelligence and the concentrated use of force.

To support productivity in the global economy, many businesses outsource their call centres to the nation of India. However, the Indian companies recognize that China can do the same work at lower cost, once language and accent training become sufficiently advanced. Meanwhile, Chinese manufacturers dominate global productivity due to low wages – a distinction once synonymous with Japanese industry. China, however, is losing some of its advantage on this front. Costs escalate with inflation, since a growing economy leads to greater prosperity and rising wage demands. Chinese manufacturers now must consider outsourcing to countries such as Indonesia, the Philippines, and Vietnam.

Innovation fulfils a similar role in modern business competition, as did Sun Tze's advanced tactics for warfare. Productivity gains are often incremental rather than revolutionary. An innovation may have the leverage to make a significant improvement in productivity, market share, or even in carving out a new market niche.

The danger in pursuing innovation is that the efforts may be misguided. By its nature, research does not have a guarantee of success; and even "successful" research can result in a product that is too expensive to compete, or one that requires an educational marketing campaign to develop a customer base.

Failing to innovate is like leaving a flank vulnerable to a land attack on a battlefield; but innovating without focus on marketability is like manoeuvring to attack where the enemy has neither troops nor assets to lose. Success comes by ensuring that the focus for innovation is on marketable products that address a growing demand at a competitive price.

Chapter 9 – EXAMPLES: MICROFINANCE AND HOME-BASED BUSINESSES

Two recent extreme trends in small business are the use of micro-financing in the third world and the rise of home-based businesses in the developed world. These two trends augur well for small busineses.

Micro-Financing as a Model for Small Business

One trend in the developing world has been the growth of micro-financing. In essence, this capitalizes an entrepreneur with a small loan. The principle is exactly that of any business that borrows money at start-up. The differences are that the loan is extremely small, the lender is neither a traditional bank nor an "angel investor", and the business owner is usually someone who otherwise would not be qualified.

A typical example would be a loan sufficient for one or two pregnant female goats, so a rural family in Cambodia, Laos or Myanmar can start a herd and also sell a bit of milk. The loan can be repaid with the first surviving offspring, so there is little risk to the lender. Usually the lender actively mentors the new entrepreneur. This helps the business succeed and also assures the lender that the collateral is still secure.

Lessons for Any Small Business

The microfinance model has lessons that can be applied by any small business. First, seek niche opportunities that have been overlooked by larger competitors. Banks cannot be bothered with such small loans. The revenue will not come near to covering the lender's costs for administrating the transaction. However, the microfinance lender has made the decision to pursue this business. It is then a matter of keeping overhead low and ensuring repayment.

The second lesson is to recognize unlikely customers or clients. A significant portion of microfinance loans go to women in societies where they otherwise have no opportunity to run their own businesses.

Recognizing viable opportunities is also important, but sometimes overlooked in discussions of micro-financing. Raising livestock, for example, is a viable option for rural families if they have access to pasture or inexpensive feed; especially if they, or their neighbours, already have some experience in animal husbandry. Another business category that often receives micro-financing is sewing, embroidery or tailoring – skills that a woman in some third world countries probably has already developed because of the culture within which she grew up. Generally, the person does not require lengthy training before launching the business. The more universal lesson is that the small business should focus on what is feasible, given the entrepreneur's skills, interests, financial backing, and estimated cash flow.

Finally, risks can be moderated by paying attention to detail. Just as the lender in a microfinance environment must keep in contact with the borrower, so must the small business owner monitor and control the details of the business. Eventually tasks might be delegated, but accountability and supervision remain necessary. It is found by many studies that the default rate on microfinance is far lower than the traditional bank and financing loans. Muhammad Yunus, the nobel peace prize winner for his microfinance work in BanglaDesh said the global economic crisis in 2008 was sparked off by non-performing loans to the big businesses and the rich. We should consider setting a banking system to lend to the poor and does not rock the world economy and the default rate is lower.

The growing popularity of micro-financing will increase the growth of small businesses.

The Growth of Home-Based Businesses

For a long time, economic activity was dominated by subsistence farming. The industrial revolution made it plain that the accumulation of capital and centralizing production in factories could lead to greater wealth, particularly for the capitalists. This pattern was to continue for as long as the need for a significant capital investment remained a barrier to production.

The low cost of, and easy access to, computers linked by the Internet have helped home-based businesses flourish. It is now possible to create intellectual property locally and disseminate it globally. Also big businesses are downsizing. Unemployed people become freelancers and start businesses at home. This is possible with the advent of internet.

Consider the music industry. It once required significant capital investment to purchase the equipment to press vinyl records. Now that music can be recorded and copied digitally, the main costs are for microphones and mixers – well within the budget of small businesses or small bands.

Likewise, previously, it had been challenging for an independent band to have their music played on commercial radio stations; and there were no other alternatives for self-promotion, other than live performances. Today, a band can start by posting videos to YouTube and "advertising" via social media such as Twitter and FaceBook.

While the economic barriers have been greatly reduced for most home-based businesses, competition is perhaps more fierce. Since "anyone" can post their music to YouTube, almost everyone does. The result is a scramble to be noticed amidst the proliferation of competitors.

Of course, home-based businesses are not limited to nascent musical groups. They simply exemplify the way the parameters of work are changing. While some businesses still require massive capital investments, others have found that it is possible to start on a shoestring budget.

A completely different example is "custom farm work". Some farmers do not take on the capital expense of a "combine harvester" that they would use for a few weeks per year. Instead, an enterprising farmer buys one and arranges to do "custom work" for his neighbours, perhaps even spending a few months travelling to harvest on many farms. That work gives a better return on the capital investment to the custom operator and costs the other farmers much less to work their fields.

China's 35,000 express delivery service companies can ship packages nearly 1000 kilometres for less than the cost of standard US letter. They completely defeat FedEx, UPS and DHL on price. These big companies only currently control less than 3 percent of the market. China is expected to overtake the $70 billion (in USD) market within two decades and therefore it is a big market potential for small delivery services. The local companies do not have the overheads of big enterprises – uniforms, big trucks or fancy gadgets. However, the local companies employ an army of home-based, package-delivering bike couriers who weave through the traffic jams as which the big trucks cannot.

The general lesson for small business is that there are opportunities to reduce costs without sacrificing effectiveness. This may allow you to conduct business from home or at lower costs by avoiding traditional expenses.

- Do you need a storefront? Why not sell online and ship to customers?

- Do you need to advertise in traditional media, such as television, radio, newspapers, or flyers? Can you reach your target market online?

- Can you outsource production? If not, could you rent equipment as needed over a short term?

- In general, have cost barriers fallen that had kept you out of a market segment? Will falling cost barriers lead to a proliferation of competitors? How will you advertise so as to be noticed by potential customers? How will you compete – in terms price, quality, or some other characteristic – when competition becomes rife?

Summary for Unconventional Opportunities

As both technology and the economy evolve, stay alert for unconventional opportunities. Some costs, such as telecommunications or data storage, are likely to keep dropping. Better tools should continue to allow amateurs to build reasonably good web sites at lower costs. Manufacturing and other business processes might be outsourced to developing countries. Other costs might continue to rise. Oil and gasoline are ultimately limited commodities and international politics are likely to cause prices to fluctuate from time to time.

You might find that your small business can gain a competitive advantage based on flexibility or proximity to your market. Tomorrow, Wal-Mart might open a store just down the highway from your village; or another multinational might find a way to deliver mass-produced goods by courier that compete with your hand-crafted artwork.

Despite the uncertainties, there is always room for the resourceful and inventive entrepreneur to create a new niche. The key is to continue looking for what your market needs that you, and preferably you alone, can provide.

Chapter 10 – VISION FOR A SUCCESSFUL SMALL BUSINESS

It has been said, "When there is no vision, the people will perish".

Consider this: if your only vision is to expand your business to be the largest in the world, you could not rest until you had defeated giants such as British Petroleum, General Motors or Apple...all of which have outlived at least one of their founders. However, you can indeed outperform a conglomerate competing on your home turf. But you won't recognize and appreciate your success if you have adopted a defeatist attitude...no matter how much money you earn or how well your business performs.

Expect and Cultivate Your Growth, both Personal and Business

Popular self-help books advise individuals to develop a vision for success. One approach is to believe in one's potential for improvement, then to work at success through diligent effort. In this situation, setbacks and obstacles provide feedback and motivation for the individual to redouble their efforts.

Personal growth is important for one's own satisfaction. Adding a new skill, broadening one's outlook, and developing an appreciation for art or culture are all ways to grow as a person. Beyond your own "

Also, put some thought and planning into improving your business. Simple improvements can change a stalemate into a victory, as a battle of chain restaurants has shown.

One Canadian success story is the Tim Horton's chain. They have kept pace with their rivals in the fast food business by expanding into niches previously occupied by local diners and the international Goliath with golden arches known as McDonald's. The fast food industry continues to ask, "What else do people eat and drink, and at what times"? Tim Horton's added at least two meals to their menu, thus building on their success that began mid-morning snacks.

Tim Horton's[19] is an example of successful business growth. Tim Horton was a professional ice hockey player in Toronto. He launched one franchised coffee-and-doughnut restaurant in 1964. Ron Joyce, the first franchise owner, became a full partner in 1967. Seven years later, there were some 40 restaurants, mainly in southern Ontario. The company has since expanded to over 3,300 restaurants across Canada, plus hundreds in the United States and a few overseas. As noted above, they expanded their offerings over the years, although they still offer their signature coffee and doughnuts. Often their menu competes with other fast food restaurants, although they have avoided the typical "hamburger". The introduction of flavoured cappuccinos may have been a response to competition from Starbucks or other premium coffee shops.

Tim Horton's also sells products. They offer their ground coffee in cans, thus allowing customers to brew their own coffee at home. Branded travel cups and stay-at-home coffee mugs offer permanent advertising as well as a profit margin.

They have found several ways to serve a varied clientele. Patrons may eat in the dining room; walk in and then take out their meals; use a drive-through service; or select from a limited menu in mini-franchises inside petrol stations, large retail stores, hospital lobbies, or other convenient locations. They are located in cities, small towns, and at many highway gasoline stations. The Tim Horton's prepaid debit card was introduced for the convenience of quick electronic payment and to avoid credit card fees for the retailer. Dedicated, self-branded pre-paid debit cards, of course, also create an effective loyalty programme. They also serve as quick, inexpensive gifts. At the time of writing, this may change if they decide to accept major credit cards.

Their early success hinged, at least in part, on the popularity and fame of the owner. Later expansion, which came after Mr. Horton's death in 1974, was based more on standard business principles: consistent quality, low prices, and marketing. As well, the company prides itself on developing ties to the local community by supporting selected charities. Advertising campaigns tend to remind customers about product quality and the broad popularity of the brand – popularity that makes Tim Horton's a safe choice when offering coffee to co-workers or casual acquaintances.

---

[19] From the Tim Horton's business site's "Biography of Tim Horton" and "Corporate Profile" pages, http://www.timhortons.com/ca/en/about/bio_timhorton.html and http://www.timhortons.com/ca/en/about/profile.html .

What lessons does Tim Horton's have for a typical small business? Several can be emulated:

- Build brand recognition. If you cannot partner with a famous local athlete or celebrity, try to advertise enough that people will learn your company's name.

- Start by catering to local demand. The original coffee and doughnuts may have been aimed at the high end of blue-collar tastes but was well within their budgets.

- Continue by outflanking the competition. Tim Horton's expanded beyond a between-meal snack to serve breakfast and lunch, and provided quick meals for people driving through the evening.

- Retain customers by building brand loyalty. Continue advertising, contribute to the community, and never disappoint past customers by discontinuing popular offerings.

- Emphasize the experience and benefits, not just product or service. Some advertising campaigns have focused on how customers have built personal relationships with strangers by sharing a coffee.

The Tim Horton's empire started small, but has grown and evolved for nearly forty years and remains an example of successful franchising.

Meanwhile at McDonald's

McDonald's remains the Goliath of fast food, but from time to time, analysts have questioned its continued success. In 1998, David Leonhardt's report[20] in *Business Week* noted a worrisome pattern of limited growth in sales and profitability.

Leonhardt began by recounting how McDonald's had previously made product changes to maintain and extend its lead in the fast food industry. The sole original restaurant served hot dogs, but a variety of hamburgers were introduced later, including the "Big Mac". Later products that succeeded included chicken nuggets, a breakfast egg sandwich, and promotional items that appeal to children.

Beyond stalling financially in the last 1990s, McDonald's also had limited or no success introducing new products although it tested many. It seems that Leonhardt was unaware of the introduction of McCafé premium coffee, as a counterattack on Starbucks. In the years since his article was published,

---

[20] David Leonhardt, "McDonald's : Can it regain its golden touch?", Business Week, March 9, 1998 at http://www.businessweek.com/1998/10/b3568001.htm .

McDonald's self-proclaimed history[21] notes a variety of reasonably successful products that expanded its brand and image. These include a fruit/yoghurt parfait, fruit smoothies, "snack wrap" sandwiches, and a specialty coffee products. Whether or not McDonald's can increase the pace of its success, it has begun to address at least one of the issues Leonhardt raised: the introduction of successful products.

Even McDonald's faces challenges in retaining customers and creating new products. However, a large corporation often has layers of bureaucracy impeding its innovators. Your small business can and should devote a larger percentage of its total efforts into innovating for its niche market.

Working at Growth

Two related methods for personal and business growth are planning and time management.

Make Flexible Plans for Your Business

Having the vision is the first step. The next adage is "Failing to plan is planning to fail". It is guaranteed that you will not reach goals that you have not set. Without timely goals and a realistic plan to achieve them, you are unlikely to succeed.

What happened to all those brave words about the flexibility inherent in a small business? Yes, it is important to adapt to changing conditions, and this flexibility is indeed a competitive advantage for smaller companies over larger ones. However, it is all too easy to slip into a pattern of doing familiar tasks for the same customers. This leads to the issue of time management.

Manage Your Time

Scientists quote Boyles' Law to say that a gas expands to fill its container. Business consultants note that work expands to fill the available time.

---

[21] "McDonald's History" at
http://www.aboutmcdonalds.com/mcd/our_company/mcdonalds_history_timeline.html?DCSext.destination=http://www.aboutmcdonalds.com/mcd/our_company/mcd_history.html .

Set a schedule that includes a realistic but challenging time to accomplish each task. Trying to do too much too quickly leads to external mistakes and emotional tension. If you have overcommitted to clients, your productivity may actually suffer as you juggle priorities.

Be sure, however, to schedule enough time for personal growth and to review and revise your business. This generally means setting priorities. It may also require that rarest of skills for a small business owner: delegation.

Delegate When Needed or Advisable

A paradox in small business is that the person who starts a business must be ready and able to handle almost every task personally, yet must begin to delegate as the workload increases. The start-up phase might be a one-person project, or include a small number of partners. There are many varied responsibilltles. To succeed, one person must accomplish a variety of tasks.

As the business grows, it may be necessary to hire staff. Will the owner successfully authorize subordinates to take over specific duties? Or will she micro-manage to the point where she cannot control the larger issues?

In a corporate environment, specialists swoop in to handle details pertaining to their own bailiwicks. A manager must delegate routine tasks to the people with the mandate to do their jobs. That manager would not be expected to input bookkeeping entries, make sales calls, fix computers, negotiate banking arrangements, and sweep the floor after closing the shop. Yet the jack-of-all-trades in charge of her own small business must do all these things and more.

The more successful she is during the start-up, the more comfortable she may feel with every detail under her own control. When the time to hire staff does arrive, it will be imperative to train and delegate. The wisest entrepreneur will begin that process before becoming frazzled with overwork. Make plans for training and also for making time afterwards to review the big picture.

As noted earlier, King David had a trusted general named Joab. Although David himself was a seasoned warrior, as king he spent part of his time ruling from his capital in Jerusalem. David delegated at least one military campaign to Joab.

Whether it was David or Joab who best understood the division of duties, they were a successful team. Joab laid siege to the city of Rabbah while David remained in Jerusalem. David did communicate with Joab during the siege. Unfortunately, the story in II Samuel 11 mainly shows that David arranged to have Uriah, one of his soldiers, killed to cover up David's affair with Uriah's wife.

Joab demonstrated the greatest wisdom in handling the delegated task of conquering the city of Rabbah. When victory was at hand, Joab summoned David to "...encamp against the city, and take it."[22] This ensured that the Israelites would praise David for the victory and it also allowed David to be the publicly visible king in Jerusalem most of the time.

Summary for Success

To succeed, the small business owner must cultivate a mind-set of success. This may not be an easy task, even for a naturally optimistic person. One obstacle is that the entrepreneur may not have the support of peers that a middle manager would develop in a corporation.

Cultivating a healthy vision may involve:

- Do cultivate relationships with your peers:
- Join a local business improvement organization, professional association or service club. These provide opportunities to network as well as a break from routine tasks.
- Join or sponsor local charitable or service activities, even if only to publicize your business.
- Attend workshops or seminars to maintain or upgrade your skills.
- Make time for important activities, such as long-term planning, recreation and personal fitness.

---

[22] II Sam. 12: 28 (KJV).

- As your business grows, discipline yourself to delegate responsibilities to your employees.

Just as running a business requires discipline, so does creating a healthy vision that allows you to succeed and to enjoy your success.

Chapter 11 – COLLABORATION IN A SMALL BUSINESS

While a sole proprietor can be a success in business, a growing enterprise requires employees, contractors or partners.

Inevitably, bringing two or more people together will create either collaboration or conflict.

Large companies have human resource departments and a corporate culture to mitigate the worst of office politics. What skills and techniques are available for the competitive small business owner?

Problems: Knocks and Blocks

One must expect internal rivals to block one's rising success, perhaps by delivering some form of a knock. In an ideal world, business partners and co-workers cooperate and collaborate to achieve success for the company, and internal rivalries are settled by displaying competence rather than by competing with allies. Since this is not an ideal world, we must be prepared for the knocks and blocks of our partners.

Mathematical Games for Cooperation and Competition

Mathematicians, particularly those working in the fields of psychology or economics, have developed "games theory" to describe how people choose to cooperate or compete.

A One-Time Opportunity: the Prisoners' Dilemma

A classic game is the "Prisoners' Dilemma". Imagine that a pair of suspects has been arrested. After being separated, each is offered a choice:

1.   If both plead "Not guilty", there is sufficient evidence for some minimal punishment.

2.   If both plead "Guilty" by turning evidence against the other, both will receive a severe sentence.

3.   If one turns evidence while the other pleads "Not guilty", the turncoat will be rewarded while the other will be very harshly punished.

If both suspects trust each other, the best overall outcome for both would to plead "Not guilty". If both believe the other to be too trusting, then the double "Guilty" plea would provide the worst overall result. However, a cunning individual will see the opportunity for the greatest personal gain by betraying the other.

A significant factor in the "game" is that the "prisoners" are not allowed to communicate with each other. If they can, it is more likely that they will try to convince each other to both plead "Not Guilty". Without negotiating, each "prisoner" must rely on their prior impressions of the other.

The "Prisoners' Dilemma" is often seen as a one-time event: the suspects would not be in this situation very frequently. When issues of trust or betrayal are repeated frequently, the partners generally work out a stable pattern. Often the first move is "trust", but a "betrayal" by the partner is punished with a follow-up "betrayal".

The Repeated Fair Offer

A game that can build trust, and which can be played repeatedly, is the "Fair Offer". One person, the "controller", is given $100 and controls the offer to the partner. The fairest offer is a 50/50 split; one expects the partner to accept such an offer. The most selfish offers are $99 for the controller, and $1 to the partner; or all for the controller with none for the partner.

However, the partner may refuse the offer. In that case, neither player receives anything. Clearly, the 100/0 offer will be rejected, since the partner would lose nothing. Economists had predicted that a rational partner would accept the $1 offer, since it is better than nothing. Almost always, however, the partner will refuse an extremely unfair offer.

If the controller knows that the game will be repeated, he can use the first few turns to negotiate with his partner. Will the partner accept $33 or $45, or refuse anything less than an even split? After an acceptable split has been determined, both players can play with minimal friction. This is especially helpful if the game allows for "as many repetitions as possible within a short time".

Of course, an unreasonable partner can also poison the well for both players. Would the controller offer $75 and accept only $25 for himself? Would you?

Applying These Games to Collaboration

Anyone might behave selfishly when presented with both an opportunity and a reward. Different people will either seek out such opportunities for small gains or resist unless the temptation is substantial. If your behaviour demonstrates that you are valuable as a long-term ally, then your partners may decide not to stab you in the back for a one-time benefit. If you show that you are trustworthy but vigilant, then you minimize the opportunities for others to harm your interests.

Three specific methods help overcome an employee's tendency to use them for selfish gain. First, consistently demonstrate that a person's efforts will be rewarded. The "Prisoners' Dilemma" experiments show that those who learn, through experience, to trust each other will cooperate rather than compete.

Second, allow some room for creativity and compromise, whether you are in the "controller" or "partner" position. Are you making fair offers or refusing to accept such?

One trick for defusing volatile situations, whether with co-workers, subordinates or customers, simply requires physically taking a position beside the other person. Picture a confrontation about a contract: the two opponents directly face each other with the document between them. Change the picture: now the two stand side by side, examining that document in front of them. That changes the dynamic from two people fighting over something into a team solving a problem together. If you change the geometry before the argument becomes so heated that you are violating the other's personal space, you have defused most of the hostility and made a win-win solution far more likely to be found.

Finally, is it absolutely necessary that your employees follow every direction to the letter? There may well be legal, safety, or health reasons for strict adherence to regulations. If so, ensure that your employees know, understand, and appreciate the importance of following the rules. However, demanding unnecessary compliance in trivial matters can result in resentment and lead to undermine your legitimate authority. Besides, do you really want to write a procedures manual for every small task?

Collaboration for David and King Saul

Chapter Three gave the illustration of David's relationship with his king, Saul. David's successful defeat of the giant Goliath, and subsequent victories over the Philistines, led to greater fame for David than for Saul. Could David have been more politically savvy? Was there any way to redirect attention back to King Saul? Was it Saul's fault for giving David too much responsibility, too quickly, and with insufficient oversight? Was David so charismatic that the people would have responded warmly to him in any case?

In Chapter 3, we also noted that King David's general, Joab, took pains to ensure that David would earn the credit for victory in a later siege. Perhaps David never did learn the lesson about being the visible leader. If he had encouraged Saul to be on hand for those early victories, (and if Saul had been available, rather than busy fighting on another front), perhaps the relationship between David and Saul might have been more beneficial to both parties.

Summary for Collaboration

Human nature leads us to take advantage of our opportunities, even when it means betraying close allies. While some people are more loyal than others, anyone might fall prey to temptation if the reward is sufficiently large. Others actively seek advantages even for minimal gains.

As a leader, one must make the effort to earn bragging rights, even if subordinates have done the heavy lifting. This also provides the ideal opportunity to graciously thank those partners and share the accolades.

When acting as a subordinate, it is vital to allow one's leaders and co-workers to share in the glory while ensuring that one's own efforts are noticed.

Remain trustworthy but vigilant.

Cultivate the attitude that you can find win-win solutions by cooperating with co-workers and subordinates. Your reputation for fair dealing may become a selling feature with your customers, too.

Chapter 12 – SUMMARY OF YOUR SMALL BUSINESS STRATEGY

Let's review the major points required for the entrepreneur to thrive in the face of competition from larger companies.

Assess Your Small Business's Competitive Situation

Even though one may dream of being the biggest fish in the largest lake, there is no reason to despair if the current reality is that you are a small fry in a small pond.

A small business can take advantage of its nature. Being small, with few layers of management, it can adapt quickly. If it caters to a single neighbourhood, the proprietor should be very familiar with local needs and regular customers. Customized service should be the rule, rather than the exception. Each employee is likely to have a broad understanding of the business.

Of course, there are disadvantages to being a small business. It is challenging to develop economies of scale or to access credit facilities. Specialized expertise must be "rented" by hiring consultants, rather than "owned" as staff employees.

Level Your Playing Field

Use the Internet like a bulldozer to level the playing field against giants. This is especially true in the realm of advertising, where content marketing and a consistent social presence can generate leads and develop prospects at a far lower cost than traditional media.

In fact, the small business owner has more credibility than a corporation when communicating online. Whether on Facebook or Twitter, a hands-on manager is more likely than a major corporation's CEO to actually handle his own messages.

As well, some small businesses can serve a global market as easily as their local neighbourhood by advertising online, communicating through e-mail and, where necessary, using shipping services.

Slay Your Giants

Your business competitors may be giants compared to your company, but it is possible to "slay" them in your local niche. One key ingredient is innovation – with a focus on profitable innovation. Many entrepreneurs find themselves drawn to either blue-sky innovation or to productivity improvements; the successful ones balance the two.

The other necessity for smaller businesses is to focus on a niche. The niche can be the local neighbourhood, personalized service, or superior quality.

Even large corporations succeed by doing well in multiple niches – more so than trying to win customers with a "one size fits all" approach. Modern consumers expect customization in many of their purchases. Starbucks is a shining example of mass customization: each order is different, yet built from standard processes by well-trained and versatile staff.

Transform Your Small Business

The Corporate Transformation process uses the analogy of treating an ailing patient with three phases called surgery, resuscitation after anaesthesia, and long-term therapy.

The first phase, surgery, cuts out unprofitable activities to reduce cost and save the business from bankruptcy. During resuscitation, the emphasis is on marketing, sales, cash flow, and profitability. The final phase, therapy, includes adjusting the corporate mind-set so that the crisis will not recur. Therapy also involves re-training a patient. In business, the emphasis shifts to disciplined innovation, enhanced productivity and the building of a cohesive team that meets customer needs while turning a profit.

As the name implies, "Corporate Transformation" was developed for large enterprises. The principles apply to small businesses as well; but with very few levels of management, it is easier to achieve success once the need for drastic action has been accepted.

Your Mind-set for Success

While a business can be profitable while remaining small, the owner's mind-set should set personal growth as a goal and also as a way of life. Tenacity is important; but most entrepreneurs either have or develop this trait by virtue of necessity.

The ability and willingness to delegate may require more discipline, but is necessary to allow the manager to devote time to management tasks. These roles include creating and planning the vision for the company's future. The owner also needs to delegate tasks, retaining only minimal supervisory control, in order to dedicate time to personal growth.

Manage or Reduce Your Office Politics

Where two or three people are gathered, they will jockey for leadership and status. While this is a fact of human nature, it need not become a destructive force. Handle office politics by rising above the fray. Look for win-win situations rather than viewing all situations as life-or-death struggles.

Remember David and Goliath

This book uses stories about David and Goliath as a reminder that "small" can defeat "large". David used his unconventional skill with a slingshot to defeat Goliath, who was the hands-down favourite to win if David had used the standard tactics of his day. Other stories about King David show that he and his friends used unconventional methods that were appropriate to their skills and situations.

Chapter 13 – Appendix I – REVIEW THE SEVEN MOUNTAINS

Reviewing these questions will assist in solidifying the concepts from the "Seven Mountains" chapter.

Questions for "Overcome Negative Mind-sets"

1. Which of the following mind-sets regarding turnaround CEOs is <u>false?</u>

    a) They strive hard to build and sustain a positive corporate philosophy.

    b) They must be ruthless and fire people in order to reduce costs.

    c) They encourage and motivate staff members in order to get the best results from them.

2. "I'm indispensable. They can't find fault with me!" What may be the cause of this common negative mind-set?

    a) Staff member being too proud of their achievements

    b) Low office standards

    c) Motivation and Encouragement by management

3. There are various ways to overcome the mind-set mentioned in question 2 above. Which of the following is <u>not</u> a good option?

    a) Start self-improvement therapy to ensure that the staff members are not complacent.

    b) Point out future tasks and challenges to prove that no one is invincible even in business.

    c) Fire the employee for being arrogant.

4. Hard work is only one basic building block of success within today's corporate world. Which other qualities are necessary?

    a) Producing good results at the right time when faced with a challenge

    b) Wearing official clothes that show a serious side of you

    c) Being friendly and getting along with everyone at the office

5. In the corporate world a lot of money is lost through assumptions. Which of the following is a <u>wrong</u> business assumption?

    a) One must protect the investments made in the past to ensure productivity.

    b) Hard work is the only quality that is required for success.

    c) Partnerships should be clearly defined on paper to avoid misunderstandings.

6. Which one of the following is a reality and not just a theory of the current state of the global corporate world?

a) There are more businesses and so more job opportunities.

b) Rising unemployment rates, downsizing, increased stress, and possibly even suicides are a reality.

c) Bank loans and grants are making businesses more sustainable.

7. Which theory regarding the Internet is <u>false</u>?

    a) The Internet makes the world a global village by interlinking us all.

    b) The Internet provides a level playing field for all businesses, whether large or small.

    c) The Internet is not a sustainable business avenue.

8. Although emotions and behaviors may indicate stress, which one group of symptoms below does <u>not</u>?

    a) Depression, anxiety, nagging worries, and lack of happiness

    b) Sleeplessness accompanied by exhaustion

    c) Relaxation and calmness with bursts of energy

9. Stress has been pointed out as a factor that reduces staff performance. How can it be reduced?

    a) Ignoring the problems causing stress and hoping that they go away

    b) Leading disciplined life with healthy food habits, plenty of fresh air and exercise, and a positive attitude

    c) Focusing on the desired end results and pray that God solves the problems

10. Prayers and meditation can give you happiness and freedom from stress.

    a) True

    b) False

    c) Both of the above

11. Which of the following exercises does not get rid of stress?

    a) Doing all the work at once to reduce tomorrow's work-load

    b) Devoting sufficient time and discipline to prayers and meditation

    c) Communing with nature and getting plenty of fresh air

12. Complete this old Chinese saying "The glory is not in ever failing, but in…………………"

    a) Failing just once

    b) Rising every time you fall

    c) Not crying when you fail

13. Which groups of people is it <u>not</u> advisable to share stress and stressful experiences with?

    a) Family, spouse, close friends

    b) Trusted relatives, therapists, and understanding neighbours

c) Strangers, enemies, and business rivals

14. Stress can be detected via physical symptoms. Which of the following is <u>not</u> a physical sign of stress?

a) Nose bleed and hair loss

b) Heartburn and chest pains

c) High blood pressure and headaches

15. How can you turnaround your own mind-set to overcome negativity?

a) Have faith in your capabilities and form a connection God for assistance.

b) Have the right culture and values; seek assistance from your friends and family when in trouble.

c) Both of the above

16. During times of failure and losses, what thought should one <u>never</u> harbour in mind?

a) This world never favours failures.

b) Very many people have made it the past by going through very harsh times.

c) Calm waters never make good sailors.

17. Defeat and setbacks are .... for achievement in life. Fill in the blank space.

a) Stepping stones

b) Corner stones

c) Gratitude stones

18. Which of the following mind-sets for entrepreneurship is <u>wrong</u>?

a) One must do what they love and enjoy doing to achieve success. Passion is therefore important.

b) If you venture out of your comfort zone you are doomed,

c) Great ideas implemented effectively and innovatively will lead to great business success

19. Corporate turnaround and personal turnaround go hand in hand for success.

a) Rarely

b) Occasionally

c) Always

20. In contrast to the industrial age, which of the qualities below characterizes a successful organization in the information age?

a) Conferences and many meetings

b) High performance with consistent innovation and productivity

c) Company cars and many employees

21. People with negative mind-sets have been known to attract negative situations. How can people in business change these mind-sets?

a) By increasing their salaries

b) By going for vacations as often as possible

c) By adopting positive thinking through prayer and meditation

22. Which of the following is not a factor that is used in the formation of various mind-sets?

a) Beliefs and desires

b) Dreams

c) Visualization and goals

23. Once an entrepreneur has the right mind-set, which other factors are equally necessary for success in business?

a) Courage and focus

b) Large amounts of money

c) Many friends and a large family

24. Contrary to popular belief, which of the following is not necessary for a successful marketing strategy?

a) Lots of money

b) A great product

c) A fool proof marketing strategy

25. The right mind-set is necessary in business since many factors are unpredictable. Which of these is an unpredictable variable?

a) What customer preferences and trends will be in the future

b) How you manage your thoughts and deal with good and bad periods

c) Your selection of business associates, coaches, mentors, and clients

26. What makes a good manager get through tough business times?

a) Talent achieved over the years

b) Education in the business field

c) A positive business mind-set

27. Which of the following companies attributes its success to simply having the right mind-set?

a) Xerox

b) Enron

c) AT&T

28. Which of the following feelings are symptoms of a positive mind-set?

    a) A lack of confidence and feelings of inadequacy

    b) Inner peace and gratitude

    c) Self-doubt and poor self-worth

29. In an effort to change the mind-sets of business individuals, a number of methods have been suggested by professionals. Which of the following is not one of them?

    a) Give what you want to get. Adopt a Givers-Gain Mind-set each day.

    b) Surround yourself with positive thinking people.

    c) Drink a lot of water and wash the negative toxins away.

30. "Leaders are made not born". Is this statement...

    a) False

    b) True

    c) None of the above

Questions for "Fly Above Office Politics"

1.   Remember the first impression you made on your colleagues when you started working? Why was this important?

    a)   The management will respect you more.

    b)   Other employees should be afraid of you.

    c)   This will really affect how you will be treated by others later on.

2.   Do you stand out in the workplace or do you always go along with what others do and say? Which one of the following statements is true about those who stand out?

    a)   If you stand out you will always be someone to blame.

    b)   If you stand out and do not have backing from a power base, you will always be involved in petty office politics.

    c)   Unproductive employees stand out.

3.   Which statement is true about team players in the office?

a) Cooperation always helps defuse office politics.

b) Educated staff members are always team players.

c) Innovation does not require team work.

4. Which of these statements is false about boundaries and respect in the office?

a) Competition tends to push boundaries of employees.

b) Lack of respect for boundaries is the only way to get success.

c) Competition fuels office politics.

5. Why should you take time to listen to your fellow employees with an open mind?

a) This is a way to avoid being criticized

b) Fellow employees know everything.

c) No one knows everything so it is always good to listen to other peoples' opinions and views while at the same time keeping an open mind.

6. How should an employee take criticism?

a) Positively. If it is genuine then use it to improve on your work.

b) Positively but only when coming from your manager.

c) Positively, if from a lady.

7. Why should you not indulge in office gossip?

a) Gossip is for after office hours.

b) Gossip can get you fired.

c) Gossip tends to aggravate relationships that definitely lead to even more politics.

8. What is the relationship between office politics and performing well and consistently in the office?

a) If you let your good consistent work speak for itself then you won't need to engage in any politics to advance yourself.

b) They go hand in hand.

c) Office politics improves the performance of staff.

9. Do you believe that minding your own business is good for your work?

a) No, because office politics are very important.

b) Yes, because keeping in the loop helps keep track of new important things you may have missed.

c) No, because it is not important to keep yourself updated.

10. Is the following statement true or false? "If you spend your life riding on someone's coattails then you are lost. You don't know which way things will blow. Bosses come and go".

a) False.

b) True.

c) This is an example of negative office politics.

11. How should you raise issues with the management?

a) Raise the issues privately with the management.

b) Share the bad news with other companies.

c) Speak or write publicly so as to cause a big scene.

12. How should employees remain professional in the work place?

a) By discussing private matters with your colleagues

b) By cutting all forms of communication

c) By drawing a fine line between personal matters and business

13. Why should employees have their own agenda?

a) To fuel office politics

b) To help contradict management

c) To help get others to easily cooperate with you

14. Employees should know their strengths and weaknesses. Why is this?

a) This assists in fuelling office politics.

b) This avoids cumbersome work.

c) This helps you work better by asking for help where you are weak and assisting others in your area of expertise.

15. Which of the following is false about constantly developing and maintaining relationships?

a) It does not matter since many people don't pay attention.

b) Being a loner makes others see you as the enemy.

c) Good relationships will help you in your career advancement.

16. Which of the following is false about being flexible in business?

a) Circumstances and situations are always changing.

b) One should stick to tried and tested methods of doing things.

c) Flowing with the wind of change will help you tremendously.

17. How should employees talk about each other in the office?

a) They should only associate with employees in the same department.

b) They should never talk to one another.

c) They should talk positively so as to improve relationships within the office.

18. Why should staff be observant?

a) Observing other people will help you understand them hence you will be able to relate better to them.

b) It's a good way to get information to gossip about.

c) It's a good way to avoid being the centre of gossip and office politics.

19. In case of a conflict should staff members take sides?

a) Always take the side of the boss.

b) Always be neutral. This will help defuse any politics that may be occurring.

c) Take the side of your friends.

20. Employees should be aware of their own, and of other people's territories.

a) They should always assume themselves to be the smartest.

b) False.

c) True.

21. Who do you approach in case of a conflict with a fellow employee?

a) Take up issues with the right authority.

b)   Be humble and let it pass.

c)   Fight for yourself.

22.   How should an employee avoid stagnating in the same position year in and year out?

a)   Be a prayerful person.

b)   Always keep moving and stay ahead even if it is only academically.

c)   Try witchcraft.

23.   Ego should not be allowed to rule your work. How can this be helped?

a)   Be humble always.

b)   Pretend to have poor communication skills so as to avoid confrontations.

c)   Use good time management.

24.   Sun Tzu likens energy to the bending of a crossbow and decision to – ?

a)   Bending the bow.

b)   Making the kill.

c)   Releasing the trigger.

25.   Which of the following is a positive office trait?

a)   Always judge others.

b)   Empathize with others.

c)   Spread rumours.

26.   As a leader which leadership qualities should you exhibit?

a)   Improving employee attitude and unity.

b)   Degrading the employees.

c)   Being bossy.

27.   Simple nice gestures go a long way in cementing relationships.

a)   False

b)   Maybe.

c)   True.

28.   Making wise decisions has a positive effect on everyone and not just you. Is the opposite also true?

a)   True.

b)   False.

c)   Both.

29.   "Concentrate on your work even when others are focusing on unimportant issues. Your work is the main reason you are in that office." What does this statement emphasize?

a)   Respect

b)   Love

c)   Focus

30.   Conflicts greatly affect the workplace atmosphere and influence the level of productivity. Who should handle these conflicts?

a)   Management.

b)   God.

c)   Staff members.

Questions for "Identify and Demolish the Bottlenecks through Transformation"

Refer to the second section of Chapter 5, "Use Transformational Processes in the Right Situations", if you are not familiar with Corporate Transformation strategies.

1.   The following are signs that a company is in dire need of transformation except...

a)   Loss of customers

b)   High profits

c)   Slow, lethargic growth

2.   The statement "One does not need to fall sick in order to get well" shows that even ___ companies are in need of transformational techniques.

a)   Relatively healthy

b)   Ailing

c)   Almost collapsing

3.   What is wrong with business schools today in relation to turnaround techniques?

a)   They produce lazy executives who rely too heavily on their subordinates.

b)   They do not teach well enough, particularly ethics and labor relations.

c)   They produce textbook executives who may be unable to cope with a crisis hence unable to transform.

4.   Turnaround executives have to be all the following except...

a)   Bossy and dictatorial.

b)   Visionaries.

c)   Crisis managers.

5.   What is one of the first steps to transformation?

a)   Changing the management

b)   Identifying the problem

c)   Curing the problem

6.   Comprehensive transformational techniques should always involve which action?

a)   Changing the corporate culture

b)   Firing employees

c)   Employing more staff

7.   Complete transformation or turnaround involves three steps. Which is the last step?

a)   Therapy

b)   Surgery

c)   Resuscitation

8.   In transformation you must treat the____.

a)   Symptoms.

b)   Disease.

c)   Root.

9.   Strengthening the corporate immune system is one of the issues involved in corporate turnaround. It includes all the following, but which one affects everyone personally?

a)   Promoting active communication

b)   Cultivating a positive mental attitude

c)   Emphasizing training and development

10. Being action oriented means being all the following except?

a)   Flexible

b)   Fast

c)   Dictatorial

11. Dr.Teng says that the main reason renowned financial institutions in America and other developed countries are on the brink of collapse is?

a)   Too many employees

b)   Their reckless lending

c)   Too many competitors

12. Unless transformational strategies are enacted, consequences of the current financial crisis could be dire. Which of the following is not among the consequences?

a)   Rising unemployment

b)   Suicidal deaths

c)   Increased profits

13. Why is "What affects America affects the rest of the world" true?

a)   We are all globally interlinked.

b)   We all dependent on America.

c)   America is the richest country.

14. In transformation stress can sometimes be a positive catalyst. How does it help?

a)   Brings out the best of us in a crisis

b)   Improves relationships

c)   Improves your health

15. Your culture and values as a leader are very important in corporate turnaround. They are useful in all the following except...

a)   Getting ahead of others

b)   Making decisions

c)   Developing credibility

16. In turnaround you have to learn several things. Which of the following is not helpful?

a)   Running away from problems is not a solution.

b)   Every problem has its own solution; you just need to find it.

c)   Some problems are too big to be solved.

17. In corporate turnaround, Dr.Teng compares the turnaround manager to a ____.

a)   A Therapist.

b)   A Doctor.

c)   A Nurse.

18.   What is one of the reasons a company reaches the need for a critical turnaround?

a)   Low sales

b)   Lazy staff

c)   Unwillingness by the management to take timely action against problems

19.   The surgical phase is part of corporate turnaround. It involves all the following except...

a)   Problem diagnosis

b)   Cost control

c)   Communication

20.   What is the main goal of the pre-transformational phase?

a)   Diagnosing the problem

b)   Treating the problem

c)   Setting the stage and creating momentum for transformation

21.   Which of the following is not a pre-transformational goal?

a)   Treat the problem.

b)   Get support.

c)   Address initial resistance to the effort.

22.   Which of the following is an indicator that transformational strategies are working?

a)   High staff morale

b)   Low sales

c)   Decreased hold on the market

23.   Removing unproductive staff and changing the corporate culture are integral parts of?

a)   Corporate transformation

b)   Employee Demoralization

c)   Business failure

24.   Two of the following are benefits of corporation transformation. Which one is not?

a)   Achievement of business plans

b)   Better employee interaction and corporate culture

c)   Wasted resources

25.   'The love of money is <u>not</u> the root of all evil'. In changing the above belief for business success, corporate transformation is necessary.

a)   False

b)   True

c)   Maybe

26.   Which of the following is the correct sequence of a successful transformation?

a)   Pre-transformational, Diagnosis, Treatment

b)   Diagnosis, Pre-transformational, Treatment

c)   Treatment, Diagnosis, Pre-transformational

27.   In corporate transformation, which of the following can<u>not</u> be classified under "Disease"?

a)   Motivated Employees

b)   Unproductive management staff

c)   Poor Corporate culture

28.   Which of the following is <u>not</u> a "Symptom" that the business requires transformation?

a)   Declining sales

b)   Big losses

c)   Profits

29.   What should a business do when it loses a lot of money?

a)   Fire the financial directors.

b)   Learn from the losses and transform accordingly.

c)   Close the business.

30.   In corporate transformation, why is there great emphasis on managers having the right belief systems?

a)   A strong spirit is necessary for effective and correct transformation.

b)   The spirit gets you feared.

c)   Managers do the work of all employees.

Questions for "Identify and Serve Your Market Niche"

1.   What is a market niche?

a)   The general market

b)   A section of the whole market on which a product or service is targeted

c)   Several market sections brought together

2.   How is a market niche created?

a)   By identifying customer needs that are not being addressed by competitors.

b)   They exist by themselves.

c)   They do not exist.

3.   What is the major concern of a market niche that a company should consider?

a)   The company's background

b)   The company's goals

c)   What the company can do for them

4.   Which of the following is a question you should ask when targeting a market niche?

a)   What problem does my product/service solve?

b)   How much profit will I earn?

c)   What if I go at a loss?

5.   In the modern world, what is the most effective way to reach a targeted market niche?

a)   By word of mouth

b)   By written media

c)   Through the internet

6.   Aggressive marketing strategies involve which approach?

a)   Using only the most popular marketing channel available

b)   Using the cheapest marketing channel available

c)   Marketing the product/service in as many effective ways as possible

7.   Which of the following is a key factor for internet marketing success?

a)   Focusing on the quantity of information on your website and not the quality

b)   A personal domain and a professional website

c)   Cost of maintaining the website

8.   Which of the following helps to effectively target a market niche?

a)   Providing instantaneous product/service delivery

b)   Using the cheapest advertising media

c)   Using false advertising to attract the market

9.   In online marketing which of the following is the most popular channel?

a)   Blogs

b)   Social websites

c)   Other websites

10.   What should a company do before pursuing a niche market?

a)   Test the market.

b)   Consult with competitors.

c)   Drop the other market niches.

11.   Which of the following is not a factor to consider when targeting a niche market?

a)   Age of the prospective customers

b)   Gender of the prospective customers

c)   Number of employees in the company

12.   In online marketing which of the following does not help you know of the effectiveness of your marketing strategies?

a)   Amount of traffic to your website

b)   The type of traffic your website attracts

c)   Amount of money you spend on the website

13.   Which of the following will improve a company's credibility to its customers?

a)   Quality product delivery

b)   Charging a lot for products and services

c)   Inconsistency in service delivery

14.   Which of the following is not a consideration in market analysis?

a)   Amount of staff needed

b)   Needs and wants of the prospective market

c)   Factors affecting the buying decisions of the prospective market

15.   A company has to keep its market updated on it products and services. Which of the following is not the best way of doing that?

a)   Monthly newsletters

b)   Word of mouth

c)   Emails

16.   An entrepreneur is targeting a small local market niche. Which is the best advertising channel to use?

a)   Internet

b)   The local newspaper

c)   The national newspaper

17. Market testing, especially in areas where there are no other competitors, is important mainly because?

a) It evaluates the cost effectiveness of working in that market.

b) All other competitors may have tried and failed.

c) It helps to know the needs of the customers.

18. What is a necessary consideration when creating a website to market your product?

a) Quality of information

b) Number of words used

c) Size of the website

19. Why is it important to ensure that your target market has a large enough customer base?

a) To outdo your competitors

b) To meet your sales target hence profit goals

c) It does not make a difference whether the market is big or small.

20. Which of the following is not an advantage of conducting a focus group to test your product?

a) A focus group helps to know the buying behavior of the market.

b) A focus group helps to know what the targeted market is in need of.

c) A focus group helps to advertise your product.

21. A company has developed a questionnaire for an online market survey. Which of the following should not be included in the questionnaire?

a) Race

b) Occupation and age

c) Household income

22. The following are ways in which you can interact with your target audience except...

a) Seminars

b) Online forums

c) Newspaper advertisements

23. If you want to sell luxury cars to a certain market, which of the following should you consider most?

a) Religion of people in that market

b) Disposable income of the people in the market

c) Gender of people in the market

24.   Which personal factor greatly affects the success of your marketing strategies?

a)   Amount of capital available

b)   Your zeal and enthusiasm

c)   Type of product you are marketing

25.   Why is it important to narrow down your target rather than generalizing?

a)   To focus your marketing on a specific group hence saving money

b)   To ensure no one else buys your product

c)   To reduce time spent on marketing

26.   The process of identifying a market is called?

a)   Marketing

b)   Feasibility study

c)   Market segmentation

27.   Quantitative consumer data is used in market research. It refers to numbers such as age, family size, and___?

a)   Gender

b)   Income

c)   Religion

28.   A company plans to open a hotel specializing in African food. Which of the following market niches should they target?

a)   An Asian community in India

b)   Immigrant Africans in America

c)   A college in Japan

29.   The following are types of market research except...

a)   Surveys

b)   Focus groups

c)   Personal selling

30.   Which of the following media channel would be most suitable for targeting a market niche found all over the world?

a)   Internet

b)   A national newspaper

c)   A local radio station

Questions for "Identify and Use the Right Productivity Tools"

1. What percentage of business problems can be cured by simply knowing what afflicts a sick business?

    a) 0%

    b) 50%

    c) 100%

2. After corporate turnaround strategies have been applied on a company which is the biggest challenge that the business faces?

    a) Maintaining profitable growth

    b) Producing a year of good financial results

    c) Growing sales faster than the National growth

3. According to the medical analogy, which term does not lead to improved productivity of a business?

    a) Therapy

    b) Resuscitation

    c) Heart Attack/Stroke

4. Which one of the following financial measurements is correct?

    a) Profitability = (Operating profit) / Turnover as a percentage

    b) Current ratio = (Current Liabilities) / (Current Assets)

    c) Stock Turnover = (Cost of Sales) * (Closing Stock)

5. Which is an obvious warning sign of impending business failure?

    a) Determining market Position

    b) Negative / Declining profitability

    c) All the above

6. Which one of the following financial measurements of productivity is false.

    a) Dividend Covers = (Profit for Fiscal year) / Dividends

    b) Quick Ratio = (Current Assets – Stocks) * (Current Liabilities)

    c) Gearing Ratio = Debt / (Debit + Equity) as Percentage

7. Which one of the following is not an external virus that can affect the productivity of business?

    a) Government Intervention

    b) Business Management Problems

    c) Changes in Consumer Behaviour

8. Productivity deals with the economics of production. Which one of the following cannot be used to measure the basic economics of production?

    a) Number of units of a product that are produced in a given time frame.

    b) Cost of production of each unit

    c) Colour and shape of the product

9. One of the following is a _false_ Productivity measure.

    a) Productivity = revenues / costs

    b) Productivity = (cost of labour and materials) / dollar value of the goods produced

    c) Productivity = Goods produced per work shift

10. Which of the viruses below, that affect the productivity of a business, is _not_ an internal virus?

    a) Natural disasters

    b) Human Resource problems

    c) Operational Costs / Weaknesses

11. Improved productivity can lead to increased profitability only if___?

    a) The market for the product remains strong.

    b) Quality of product is maintained.

    c) Quantity of the product is maintained.

12. Communication is essential in the turnaround process. Which one of the following is _not_ part of the turnaround communication process?

    a) Write a list of staff members to be fired.

    b) Form a turnaround team and enlist support.

    c) Apply a no-nonsense management style.

13. In the surgical phase of improving productivity what do the 4 C's stand for?

    a) Communication, Cost Control, Cash Flow and Cash Cow

    b) Cash Flow, Communication, Career and Concentration

    c) Communication, Cost Control, Cash Flow and Concentration

14. _Before_ downsizing the workforce, what should management do?

    a) Make employees feel guilty and worthless.

    b) Evaluate each staff member's qualities and motivate the staff to give their best.

    c) Focus only on costs that the business stands to cut by cutting down the workforce.

15. Which option is _not_ an alternative to firing staff?

    a) Implementing pay cuts

b) Using part-timers instead of full – time staff only

c) Causing harm to staff so as to get insurance benefits

16. Which of the following measures during the corporate turnaround is not a temporary measure?

a) Cutting Perks and Benefits

b) Firing all staff members and getting a new team of staff members

c) Combining various job functions

17. In the medical analogy, Benign Tumors have been referenced and described. With this in mind, which of the following types of staff members is the odd one out?

a) Self-driven and innovative staff

b) Incompetent staff

c) Unmotivated and lazy staff

18. What are malignant tumor cases?

a) Staff that cannot find alternative employment

b) Dysfunctional groups of personnel with negative attitudes working against the interests of the company

c) Staff members that are counterproductive but valuable to the business

19. Which one of the following is not a goal of corporate turnaround?

a) Plug any holes that are bleeding and avoid further debts.

b) Bring the company back to a breakeven or profitable position.

c) Fire as many employees as possible to increase profits.

20. Company accounts are crucial for the success of any business. Which of the following is not a good accounting practice?

a) Establish credit terms in writing to customers.

b) Threaten Customers & Creditors for the best credit terms.

c) Make calls on overdue accounts and take legal action where necessary.

21. Select one of the productivity measures for sales effectiveness that is false.

a) Sales turnover = No. of resignations / No. of employees

b) Sales Performance = Total sales / No. of Employees

c) Total Sales = No. of Employees / Individual sales performance

22. The technical Energy Performance = No of items Produced / Energy Required. Based on this, and assuming that the energy required per item remains constant regardless of the number of items produced, which of the following is true?

a) An increase in No. of Items produced will reduce the energy required.

b) A reduction in No. of items produced will reduce energy required.

c) Energy performance will be increased when Energy required is increased.

23. "Successful companies must grow new businesses. That is what leads to sustained profitable growth.'' Who said these words?

a) Jack Welch

b) Dr. Mike Teng

c) Mehrdad Baghai

24. What is not necessary for a successful marketing strategy?

a) A lot of money

b) A great product

c) A fool-proof marketing strategy

25. It is _____ critical to compare your organization's productivity measurements against industry standards and your closest competitors.

a) Always

b) Never

c) Sometimes

26. In improving the quality of a product, which of the following is not necessary?

a) Make short term changes in product mix, pricing, and marketing.

b) Determine objectives, noting market opportunities and competitor's positions.

c) Lay the foundation for your product and neglect strengthening of brand and new business opportunities.

27. The quality of a product can be measured as a percentage of non-defective products relative to all products. Which of these metrics cannot be used to measure this?

a) Size and colour of the products produced

b) Cost of inputs

c) Value of outputs

28. Which factor is not important for success when a business is using the internet to grow?

a) A professional website to grow with good quality content

b) Random pop-up messages

c) Online presence and a good marketing strategy

29. Who said that "you can't control what you can't measure" in "Controlling Software projects: Management, Measurement and Estimation"?

    a) Jack Welch

    b) Barack Obama

    c) Tom DeMarco

30. Which of the following is <u>not</u> an internet productivity ratio?

    a) Views per day and visitors per day

    b) Website hosting charges

    c) Contact and sales conversion rate

Questions for "Innovate to Outsmart the Competition"

1.   Which of the following is the <u>least</u> innovative use of the Internet for a small business?

    a) The site includes requests and results for customer feedback, with voting and comments.

    b) The site includes customer registration to receive e-mails with special offers.

    c) The site includes contact information, location, hours of business, a selection of customer testimonials and an overview of the types of goods sold.

2.   Only by pursuing the twin goals of productivity and innovation can a company gain and retain a competitive edge.

    a) False

    b) True

    c) Both

3.   Which of the following criteria is <u>not</u> necessary for the cultivation of an innovation culture?

    a) Rules and regulations: innovative companies strike a balance between flexibility and enforcement.

    b) Smart staff and geniuses: a company must invest in very smart staff members and do away with all the average and below average staff members.

    c) Problem Finders: people who notice bottlenecks and set out to make improvements.

4.   What should a company do after a <u>failed</u> attempt at innovation?

    A.   Punish the individual responsible and make an example out of them.

    b) Use this as a learning experience and find out what they did wrong to avoid a recurrence.

    c) Despair and stick to tried and tested formulae.

5.   Creativity must be _____ in an innovative organization.

a) Nourished

b) Forbidden

c) Discouraged

6.   Which condition is critical for a company to encourage innovation?

a) The company must have a lot of money to spend.

b) Resources for innovators: the organization must provide resources to support innovation.

c) Investors who are willing to pour in money.

7.   Which of the qualities below does not characterize a successful organization?

a) High performance

b) Consistent innovation and productivity

c) Many new employees

8.   A company's leadership should be at the forefront in encouraging innovation. Which of the statements is false?

a) A mature company has established systematic processes to ensure the best outcomes in each endeavor.

b) A company should rely solely on tried and tested products and processes.

C.   A company must provide an environment that encourages creativity.

9. What should a company do when their competitors come up with new products that render theirs obsolete?

A.   Start false rumours to discredit the product.

b) Apply innovation and productivity to remain relevant.

c) Start a new business.

10. Innovation often has failures before success as illustrated by the famous inventor, Thomas Edison. What was his answer when asked how he managed to keep trying after a thousand times of failure?

a) I prayed a lot and trusted God.

b) I knew that fire was not the only source of light and so I kept trying.

c) It was not a few thousand times of failure but rather a few thousand steps to the right solution.

11. Which of the following is a false measure of innovation?

a) Annual gross innovations (AGI) per employee= Number of innovations suggested per year / number of employees (head count)

b) Annual implemented innovations (AII) per employee= Number of innovations implemented per year /   by the number of employees (Head count)

c) Annual implemented innovations (AII) per employee= Number of Innovations implemented per year * the number of employees (Head count)

12. What is a Staff Satisfaction Index (SSI)?

a) An index which measures employee satisfaction and engagement in the workplace

b) An index which measures management's satisfaction with the employees

c) An index which measures Customer satisfaction in staff performance

13. Which is the latest tool for a business seeking to reach their customers and clients more innovatively?

a) FAX

b) Internet

c) Bluetooth

14. Which of the following is least important when it comes to internet marketing?

a) A server to host the web site

b) A fool-proof marketing strategy

c) A great product and a website specifically developed to sell the product

15. Which role is mostly played by Singapore small medium sized companies?

a) Producer

b) Middleman

c) Consumer

16. Which of the following statements is true?

a) Innovation is more important that productivity.

b) Productivity is more important that innovation.

c) Productivity and innovation have to go hand in hand for success.

17. Which year did Trek Technology and IBM begin selling the first USB flash drives commercially, as a new innovation?

a) 2000

b) 1998

c) 2004

18. Which should a company prioritize to gain and retain a competitive edge?

a) Productivity

b) Innovation

c) Both should be pursued, in balance

19. "What Singapore needs most is not increasing productivity or innovation alone but improving productivity innovatively and innovation productively shall be the key thrust for our economy." Who said these words?

    a) Sun Tzu

    b) Fan Zeng

    c) Dr. Mike Teng

20. Which was the thesis presented by Michael Treacy and Fred Wiersema, in their book *The Discipline of Market Leaders*?

    a) Those successful companies – the market leaders – excel at delivering one type of value to their chosen customers.

    b) Market leaders ensure that they crush their competition and get the customers.

    c) Customers are always going to buy products from the market leaders.

21. The Turnaround CEO has to reorient the company's philosophy. Which of the following tenets should he not bear in mind during this process?

    a) Maintain a safety net in case things don't work out.

    b) New ideas and ways of doing things and acceptance of change as a constant.

    c) Be willing to accept failure as a result.

22. Fill in the blank in the statement below. "It is important for the company to _____ remind itself of this cornerstone corporate philosophy to ensure that there is no substantial deviation or omission along its corporate journey".

    a) Rarely

    b) Occasionally

    c) Periodically

23. Which of the following is a noble value of corporate philosophy?

    a) Unethical code of conduct

    b) Responsibilities to society and environment

    c) Disrespect for the individuals

24. What can be defined as a business innovation?

    a) Something different that is bound to have a great business impact

    b) A brand new business

c) A business that has merged to form a bigger business

25. Which is the main reason why businesses do not get the breakthrough they all want with new innovations?

    a) Fear of failure

    b) Comparative implementation of innovations

    c) Failure to implement innovations productively

26. In the service industry, success lies in feedback on the innovation.

    a) Maybe

    b) False

    c) True

27. In getting the right business culture, we have been told that the heart needs to be in the right place for success. Based on this which of the following statements is false?

    a) Let your heart be right, it does not matter where the head lies.

    b) As a man thinks in his heart so is he.

    c) Always listen to your head, not your heart.

28. Office politics have been known to hinder innovative business ideas. How can the turnaround CEO make sure this does not get in the way of success?

    A.   Take each employee to therapy beforehand.

    b) Focus on individual success of each employee and the good of the organization.

    c) Give orders and ensure that all staff members follow without fail.

29. Twitter is acclaimed as one of the most productively implemented innovation. Who was the founder?

    a) Jack Dorsey

    b) Mark Zucherberg

    c) Bill Gates

30. Which has been pointed out as the starting point for innovation in the 21st century?

    a) Whatever the market demands

    b) The latest company products

    c) Research and development based on past successful products

Questions for "Take Action"

1. According to Dr.Teng, which is the main reason why companies fail?

    a)   Management fails to take the right action at the right time

    b)   Overspending

    c)   Office politics

2.   Taking the right action to find out what the problem is in a company helps to___?

    a)   Find someone to blame.

    b)   Ensure the same problems do not occur again.

    c)   Sack unproductive employees.

3.   What action has Google taken to avoid collapse in the current economic crisis?

    a)   Put more capital into its business.

    b)   Employ more educated staff.

    c)   Foster innovation and take calculated risks.

4.   Which action should be taken first on an ailing company?

    a)   Surgery

    b)   Diagnosis

    c)   Therapy

5.   Business schools today are unable to produce executives who are able to take the right action during a crisis. Why is this so?

    a)   They lack funds for training.

    b)   They don't teach long enough.

    c)   They only rely on textbook knowledge.

6.   Taking the right action does not only mean doing something but also doing something with the purpose to...?

    a)   Achieve a goal.

    b)   Get more profits.

c)   Not feel guilty.

7.   The acronym A.C.T is used to explain the meaning of 'right action' in business. What does the second letter stand for?

a)   Calculate your losses.

b)   More Capital input.

c)   Calculate your next steps.

8.   Which of the following represents the letter A in the acronym A.C.T?

a)   Assess your risks.

b)   Calculate your next steps.

c)   Tap into your resources.

9.   To come up with an action plan for resuscitating a company which of the following is not a question to consider?

a)   Who is to blame?

b)   What didn't work and why?

c)   What are our goals?

10.   What went wrong in the IBM Company in the 1990s although it had skilled management?

a)   Employee strikes

b)   A corporate culture of arrogance and ignoring the threat of personal computers

c)   Negative office politics

11.   Treatment to eradicate external viruses in a business helps to___?

a)   Foster a strong and healthy corporate culture.

b)   Spread the viruses to other companies.

c)   Increase the internal viruses.

12.   The surgical phase in corporate turnaround comprises all the following actions except?

a)   Cost control

b)   Communication

c)   Lowered production

13.   Key actions in enhancing communication in a business should include all the following except?

a)   Enlisting support

b)   Applying a no nonsense management style

c)   Being dictatorial

14.   Dr. Teng characterizes measures applied in business surgery to medical actions. Which of the following measures is not correctly matched?

a)   Changing managers-Blood transfusion

b)   Closing down some operations-Blood letting

c)   Change of business models-Sewing up wounds

15.   Which of the following helps to reduce costs?

a)   Not providing chauffeurs

b)   Providing first class air tickets

c)   Having frequent company retreats

16.   Which of the following actions helps to increase focus in a business?

a)   Multitasking

b)   Eliminating marginally profitable projects

c)   Delegating tasks

17.   Which of the following does not help in cost control?

a)   Creating a realistic budget

b)   Downsizing the workforce

c)   Increasing employment

18.   Two of the following are alternatives to firing staff. Which one is not?

a)   Forced retirement

b)   Pay cuts

c)   Perks and benefits reductions

19.   Cash flow management involves all the following except?

   a)   Building up the cash reserves

   b)   Increasing spending

   c)   Utilizing the cash wisely

20.   What action did the Neptune Orient Line take during the Asian financial crisis in 1997 and 98?

   a)   Downsized the workforce

   b)   Controlled cost

   c)   Sold off loss making and non-core assets

21.   Which action can be taken to ensure that debtors do not hurt a business?

   a)   Take legal actions where necessary.

   b)   Do not offer credit at all.

   c)   Offer credit only to a few select people.

22.   Although a company has an excellent vision it may still collapse due to___?

   a)   Having the wrong vision.

   b)   Implementing action slowly and inflexibly.

   c)   Taking the wrong actions.

23.   Action has to be accompanied by vision and___.

   a)   Feedback.

   b)   Communication.

   c)   Good management.

24.   Sun Tzu likens energy to the bending of a crossbow and decision to___?

   a)   Notching the arrow onto the string.

   b)   Making the kill.

   c)   Releasing the trigger.

25.   Communication breakdown in a company may lead to all of the following except?

a) Misunderstanding

b) Improved morale

c) Rumour mongering

26. Which of the following is important in cultivating a positive mental attitude?

a) Improving employee attitude

b) Degrading the employees

c) Being bossy

27. An action driven orientation involves all the following except?

a) Quick implementation of the right strategies

b) Flexibility of the corporate culture

c) Slow action implementation

28. Which of the following actions can be applied personally to increase productivity within the company?

a) Getting more rest and recreation

b) Overworking

c) Encouraging employee feedback

29. An example of a company that thrives on fast and flexible action implementation is___?

a) Apple

b) Dell

c) Hewlet Packard (HP)

30. When preparing an action plan, one of the most important things to do is___?

a) Prioritize.

b) Make it long.

c) Do not be quick in implementing it.

Answers to "Overcome Negative **Mind-sets**"

Question	Answer	Notes
1	B	Turnaround CEOs do more than ruthlessly eliminate staff.
2	A	Pride suggests "I'm indispensable"
3	C	Firing proud employees will not improve them.
4	A	Delivering under pressure is vital; the others are nice.
5	B	Another quality beyond "hard work" include adaptability.
6	B	Mergers, consolidations and business failures also occur. Loans will not float businesses forever, especially when conditions tighten.
7	C	People will continue to communicate and engage in commerce. Any one Internet company or business model might be superseded, however.
8	C	This seems obvious.
9	B	The 'B' package should work for anyone. Believers might find success with 'C', but it would be difficult to apply to all.
10	A	Prayer and meditation work for those who follow the practices. Again, it would be difficult to impose this on all employees.
11	A	Doing everything at once is more stressful; and tomorrow will have new problems.
12	B	This saying puts the emphasis on persistence.
13	C	Rivals may use the information against you.
14	A	Chronic stress raises blood pressure but not to the point of nose bleed. The symptoms, if any, are usually found in the torso.
15	C	Either or both are useful.
16	A	Both 'B' and 'C' can be comforting; but "failure" is a temporary condition.
17	A	Use the setbacks as part of the path, and leave them behind. "Cornerstones" are prominent parts of a building; don't highlight the defeats.
18	B	Personal and business growth can be achieved by extending the comfort zone.
19	C	Both are important. Both small and large businesses identify with the CEO.
20	B	Both 'A' and 'C' may be symptoms of bloated bureaucracies.
21	C	A is temporary, and B is not feasible. C can work but does depend on the individual since it cannot be mandated.

22	B	Dreams are idle flights of fancy; the others imply planning and purposeful action.
23	A	A: The leader must possess these traits. B: No; this book discusses ways to succeed with a limited budget. C: No; a strong social support network is nice but not a business requirement.
24	A	Frugal marketing can use the Internet, word of mouth, press releases...
25	A	Even continued market research cannot predict tomorrow's trend. However, you yourself influence, if not fully control, 'B' and 'C'.
26	C	Education and talent may be superseded by changes in the business environment.
27	A	Xerox did say this.
28	B	This is the only positive choice.
29	C	Drinking water may have physical health benefits, but we're focussed on mind-set.
30	B	Leadership skills can be learned and improved though practice.

Answers to "Fly Above Office Politics"

Question	Answer	Notes
1	C	If you begin and consistently behave well towards others, they will reciprocate. If you become inconsistent, others will reduce their respect for you.
2	B	You want to be "outstanding" for your skills and solid performance. Being disagreeable or slacking off will get you noticed...in the wrong way.
3	A	Anyone may jockey for position. Innovation requires multiple skills.
4	B	Respect the other person's authority; cooperate for mutual benefit.
5	C	Wisdom is derived from a sharing of insights and viewpoints.
6	A	Co-workers, customers and suppliers may offer valid and constructive criticism.
7	C	If you belittle others behind their backs, eventually they may retaliate.
8	A	A: Yes, at least with minimal politics. B: No, it is too tempting to play politics to compensate for poor performance. C: No, workers tend to be distracted by office politics.
9	A	You do need to be aware of office politics, without being a protagonist.
10	B	The emphasis is on directing oneself (while achieving corporate goals).

11	A	This is the best hope of maintaining healthy relationships.
12	C	The other choices are extremes that harm healthy working relationships.
13	C	Of course you want the best for yourself; be open so it can be a win-win.
14	C	This helps build and maintain constructive relationships.
15	A	People will notice if you are a loner.
16	B	External circumstances change, so "adapt or perish".
17	C	The other choices are extremes that harm healthy working relationships.
18	A	This is the only positive reason.
19	B	The other choices are extremes that harm healthy working relationships.
20	C	This shows healthy respect. Also, remember the Golden Rule.
21	A	If you couldn't solve the problem amicably, seek an appropriate referee.
22	B	Further education may help you volunteer for a new challenge.
23	A	Humility, or appropriate humble behaviour, counteracts egotism.
24	C	In archery, one draws the bow, aims, and then releases.
25	B	The other choices are negative.
26	A	Leadership evokes the best efforts and results from others.
27	C	However, 'B' would be correct if the gestures are insincere or inconsistent.
28	A	Your bad decisions will lead others to mistrust you and your judgement.
29	C	The key words are "concentrate" and "focus".
30	A	The question assumes the conflict has escalated beyond the co-workers' ability to resolve.

Answers to "Identify and Demolish the Bottlenecks through Transformation"

Question	Answer	Notes
1	B	A dwindling customer base and stagnant growth indicate the need for transformation.
2	A	Both 'B' and 'C' obviously need help.
3	C	Turnaround situations may follow patterns, but are not simply math exercises.
4	A	Lead by inspiration, not by terrorism.
5	B	One must diagnose before treating a disease.
6	A	Simply reducing headcount will not correct other problems, but the cash flow would not support more staff if the company needs to turn around.
7	A	Think of "therapy" as rehabilitation and retraining.
8	C	This is like making a habit of eating wisely as part of a weight loss program.
9	B	Both 'A' and 'C' are more oriented to groups; 'B' is more internal to each person.
10	C	Dictators might be obeyed through fear, but you cannot always micromanage.
11	B	Both 'A' and 'C' may cause chronic problems, but risky loans can create an acute crisis in very short order.
12	C	Lead by inspiration, not by terrorism.
13	A	As the Eurozone crisis of 2012 has shown, even small economies such as Greece can affect markets around the world.
14	A	Stress, at the levels found during corporate transformation, is not conducive to better health; nor does it leave much energy for social relationships.
15	A	The turnaround leader must gain support by working toward common goals.
16	C	It's not helpful to say that a problem is "too big". Try breaking it up, instead.
17	B	The doctor has overall authority and responsibility.
18	C	Often the "crisis" should have been recognized and treated in its infancy.
19	A	Diagnose before treating.
20	C	Begin capturing minds and hearts in the pre-transformational phase.
21	A	Diagnose before treating.
22	A	Of course, 'B' and 'C' are symptoms of the problem, not of the solution.

23	A	Reducing headcount is not a complete solution, but may be necessary for it.
24	C	Transformation should find better ways to use resources, or to stop using them.
25	B	Unrestrained greed has caused some crises; embezzlement is one example.
26	B	The exact pre-transformational strategy depends on the diagnosis.
27	A	This is the positive.
28	C	This is the positive.
29	B	The other options do not lead to solving the not-yet-analyzed problem.
30	A	Transformation requires personal energy, or "spirit".

Answers to "Identify and Serve Your Market Niche"

Question	Answer	Notes
1	B	A "niche" is only one segment.
2	A	Identify a cluster of needs that one can address.
3	C	Plan to meet the customers' needs.
4	A	Plan to meet the customers' needs.
5	C	Unless your niche is a remote tribe; then consider cell phones.
6	C	The key word is "aggressive".
7	B	Don't expect a free web site that supports amateur bloggers to be an effective marketing tool. Invest in your own domain name, professional appearance and, if necessary, a ghost writer. When using social media such as Facebook, consider hiring a professional to set up the corporate page, and be sure to update and "engage" regularly.
8	A	Meet your customers' needs as quickly and reliably as possible. Customers in a niche market probably have difficulty finding what they want.
9	B	Market your product or service by promotions via social media. Use a web site to present reference information, such as product lists.
10	A	Be sure that there is a market for this product before committing to expenses.

11	C	You can target a niche market with few or many employees, depending on what it takes to create, deliver and market the product.
		While age and gender might differentiate your customers, there is no barrier to marketing to specific ages.
12	C	The number of visitors, and what they do, indicate effectiveness.
		The amount spent is simply an input.
13	A	Quality results in long-lasting credibility.
14	A	If the demand is there, then you can calculate the price to cover your personnel.
15	B	Word of mouth is effective in passing customer opinion about their past experiences. This question relates to news "updates", so you must be pro-active.
16	B	The key phrase is "local market".
17	B	The competition may have already failed to arouse market interest.
18	B	Quality is critical.
19	B	One cannot possibly make enough sales if the market is too small.
20	C	A focus group is far too small to "advertise" a product.
21	A	Ask for "age" and "income" ranges, not for specific numbers.
22	C	The key word is "interact". Newspapers only communicate in one direction.
23	B	Selling luxury goods necessitates a clientele with sufficient disposable income.
24	B	The key word is "personal".
25	A	The key word is "narrow down"; this can take extra time to do properly.
26	C	This is identifying the segment of a market most likely to buy the product.
27	B	The key word is "quantitative": dealing with a numeric value.
28	B	B: The only group certain to have an interest in this product.
29	C	While you might learn something during a sales call, market research elicits information from groups, and does not try to make sales.
30	A	This is the only single channel with international reach.
		The others would require separate campaigns in each market.

Answers to "Identify and Use the Right Productivity Tools"

Question	Answer	Notes
1	B	The other percentages are too extreme to be reasonable.
2	A	Corporate Turnaround might be seen as a one-time project.
3	C	'A' and 'B' are treatments; a heart attack is a disease.
4	A	Neither 'B' nor 'C' should have costs or liabilities in the numerator.
5	C	Both 'A' and 'B' are warning signs.
6	B	A "ratio" requires division, but 'B' simply multiplies.
7	B	Management is internal; government and consumers are external.
8	C	Colour and shape do not affect the cost, especially compared to the others.
9	B	Productivity in general is "result / effort"; 'B' is inverted.
10	A	Natural disasters come from the outside environment. The others are sourced internally.
11	A	Lower quality may reduce consumer demand, but profits might be maintained. Saving a weekend shift bonus but reducing total output might maintain profits. But if the demand for an item wanes, no productivity improvement can make up for a total lack of sales.
12	A	Both 'B' and 'C' are positive forms of communication.
13	C	A "cash cow" is a business division with high profits, needing no reinvestment. One's career is not a factor for the company's productivity.
14	B	The goal is to retain those who will contribute to the company's success; and also to motivate them to do so.
15	C	This is both illegal and immoral.
16	B	Both 'A' and 'C' could be reversed if conditions improve.
17	A	This is a positive, not a negative.
18	B	These people actively cause problems.
19	C	Reducing headcount might be a possible means towards the goal. It certainly is not the goal unto itself.
20	B	To "threaten" goes well beyond good receivables management, per 'C'.

21	C	Productivity in general is "result / effort"; 'C' is inverted.
22	B	'A' might be true for, say, baking more loaves of bread in a pre-heated oven. 'B' is correct under the stated assumption. Think of using an arc welder. 'C' decreases efficiency by increasing the input of energy used.
23	C	This is the person who said it.
24	A	This book suggests ways to market effectively within a reasonable budget.
25	A	It is too easy to be complacent with one's current productivity.
26	C	The key problem is "neglecting" marketing.
27	A	Higher cost/unit or lower value/unit might indicate more defective products were being scrapped, or blemished products were sold at a discount.
28	B	Pop-up messages tend to annoy consumers rather than to motivate sales.
29	C	This is the person who said it.
30	B	Productivity is a ratio of "benefit / cost"; by itself, a "cost" is not a ratio.

Answers to "Innovate to Outsmart the Competition"

Question	Answer	Notes
1	C	This information is basic and important, but remains static; it neither builds nor maintains the customers' attention over time.
2	B	"True" does mean the "twin goals". "Both" is redundant but not wrong.
3	B	Average people can contribute to an innovation culture.
4	B	Some innovation attempts will not succeed; but the next might.
5	A	'A' is the only positive; creativity and innovation are indeed related.
6	B	Innovation requires some investment; 'A' and 'C' imply large amounts.
7	C	Especially if high employee turnover is the reason for new employees.
8	B	This describes the opposite of an innovative company.
9	B	'A' is immoral and may lead to a lawsuit. 'C' is creative but is more difficult and time consuming.
10	C	Edison was persistent and knew his process was making progress.

11	C	This multiplies innovations times employees; it should divide.
12	A	SSI measures how satisfied the staff members are.
13	B	FAX is an older technology. Bluetooth connects one pair of devices.
14	A	It is relatively easy to buy or rent a server.
15	B	The middleman buys from producers and resells to consumers.
16	C	Balancing the two is key.
17	A	2000 was the date.
18	C	Both are required.
19	C	That's the person who said this.
20	A	That's what they said.
21	A	One cannot maintain a "safety net" while making these radical changes.
22	C	This implies a disciplined and scheduled review process.
23	B	Only 'B' is "noble".
24	A	'A', because it is implicitly an innovation "within" a specific business.
25	C	The failure is usually due to poor implemenation.
26	C	Feedback is vital: how do the customers or clients like the innovation?
27	C	Only 'C' puts the emphasis on the "head", which contradicts the quotation.
28	B	'A' is not feasible, and 'C' may lead to mutiny.
29	A	That's the person who implemented Twitter.
30	A	Determine what the market will want next, and deliver it well and quickly.

Answers to "Take Action"

Question	Answer	Notes
1	A	Management has the responsibility to monitor and respond in a timely fashion.
2	B	Only 'B' seeks the root cause of a problem.
3	C	Google is famed for innovation.
4	B	Diagnose the problem before trying to solve it.
5	C	Few crises follow textbook examples.
6	A	The right action is goal-oriented, but this may look beyond short-term profits.
7	C	'C' is forward-looking.
8	A	Only 'A' uses the initial letter 'A'.
9	A	Blaming an individual reduces morale and hinders making innovative improvements.
10	B	IBM failed to recognize the potential for growth in the PC market; and they had succeeded brilliantly in the enterprise computing market.
11	A	Removing a virus improves health.
12	C	Surgery uses "4 Cs". Reducing production might be a correct action in some situations, but is not part of the regular surgery phase.
13	C	'B' still seeks input and advice; 'C' only commands.
14	C	"Sewing up wounds" is not one of the medical images.
15	A	Only 'A' reduces costs.
16	B	Multitasking diffuses an individual's focus. Delegating tasks does improve the manager's focus, but the question relates to the focus for the overall business.
17	C	Increased headcount might increase production levels, but does not control costs.
18	A	Forced retirement still moves people out of the workplace. 'B' and 'C' reduce costs while maintaining staffing levels.
19	B	Increasing spending when cash flow is restricted, is a sign of poor cash flow management.
20	C	They put their focus on their profitable core business.
21	A	Both 'B' and 'C' reduce sales.

22	B	The other options imply having poor vision.
23	A	Both 'B' and 'C' are intrinsic to taking action, but some may neglect 'A'.
24	C	"Decision" is the action by the archer after summoning the energy.
25	B	Poor communication always harms morale.
26	A	Only 'A' is a positive action.
27	C	"Slow" is the opposite of "action-driven".
28	C	The others harm productivity: either right away, or in the long term.
29	A	They have regular (and well publicized) product update cycles.
30	A	The others are detrimental.

Chapter 14 – OTHER RESOURCES FROM DR. TENG

Appendix II – Online Resources For Chapter 3 "HOW SMALL BUSINESS CAN CLIMB SEVEN MOUNTAINS"

These online resources by Dr. Mike Teng cover the seven tactics whereby a small business can climb the "seven mountains".

Tactic 1: Overcome Negative Mind-sets

Additional resources

1. Turn Yourself Around: How to get out of depression during the second great depression

www.turnaroundyourself.com

This unique book can get you back on track so that you are happy, healthy and emotionally stable again.

2 . Inspirational Notebook

www.inspirationalnotebook.com

A book to inspire and encourage companies for corporate transformation and turnaround with poems, Youtube videos and books outlines. A good companion to have for one's note-taking as well.

3. Jesus: The Corporate Turnaround Expert

www.corporateturnaroundexperts.com

Know how Jesus was able to change the 12 disciples' lives from simple fishermen and tax collectors into great leaders and preachers in just THREE YEARS.

Tactic 2: Fly Above Office Politics

Additional Resources

1.   What we can learn from the animals about office politics

(www.officepolitic.com)

Often, playing office politics can make you feel like you are navigating in a dangerous jungle, jumping one obstacle only to discover that a predator is on your tail. It's no wonder that the animals that navigate the real jungle might have some insight for us office-predators and office-prey.

2.   Office Politics Mania

(www.officepoliticmania)

This book uses cartoons to illustrate the craziness of things taking place in offices today. It helps reader to laugh at the realities of office politics.

3.   What we can learn from the Bible about office politics

 (www.changeorganisation.com)

   The reader can learn from the Bible on how to handle office politics. Biblical characters such as Peter, Paul, David, and Moses adeptly handled the politics of their times.

Tactic 3: Identify and Demolish the Bottlenecks through Transformation

Additional Resources

1. Corporate Wellness: 101 principles in turnaround and transformation and other transformation package

www.corporateturnaroundexpert.com

"Increase Your Profits by 107% in 9 months Using 27 years of Time-Tested East-West Strategies using 3 Simple Steps."

2. Training Manual: Corporate turnaround and transformation Methodology

www.turnaroundmethodology.com

A comprehensive and ultimate corporate turnaround methodology that melds best practices from the West and the East, soundly transforming troubled Companies into industry leaders.

3. Corporate Wellness: Spiritual and secular principles in corporate turnaround and transformation

www.turnaroundservice.com

By understanding the principles contained in this book, you can save your company – it's as simple as that! Don't wait until you're filing for bankruptcy to believe that corporate wellness is the foundation from which the success of a company is built.

4. Corporate Turnaround: Nursing a sick company back to health
www.miketeng.com
Using medical analogies, Corporate Turnaround: Nursing a Sick Company Back to Health prescribes effective and easy-to-administer turnaround techniques in the right doses

5. Turnaround Handbook: Corporate Turnaround and Transformation
www.turnaroundhandbook.com
This is a very comprehensive handbook on corporate transformation and turnaround. It provides other online resources that the reader can turn to for guidance. These resources include ebooks, Youtube videos, and poems on transforming corporations. The handbook guides the reader on corporate transformation and turnaround at the strategic, tactical, and individual levels.

6. Transformation Toolkit: Corporate Transformation to improve Productivity and Innovation
www.transformationtoolkit.com
The "Transformation Toolkit: Corporate Transformation to Improve Productivity and Innovation" provides the means to diagnose an ailing business organization, and then plan and pursue the steps to keep it alive and make it healthy.

7. Business Diagnosis

www.restructuringcosts.com

This book provides a guide on how to determine corporate health. It also provides a list of cost-cutting measures to help company manage its cash flow.

Tactic 4: Identify and Serve Your Market Niche

Additional Resources

1. Internet Turnaround: The use of internet marketing to turn around Companies

www.turnaroundinternet.com

"Internet Turnaround" is a step-by-step guide that will enable you to discover the rules of winning in the internet business.

2. Link Baiting to improve your page rank on search engines

www.linkbaitings.com

Link Baiting survives as the most productive marketing tool for Internet and SEO marketing. It has transformed this internet marketing tool into a fully established form of attracting visitors and increasing rankings.

3. The ultimate internet marketing strategies and tactics during turbulent times.

www.ultimateinternetstrategy.com

This book gives an update on what is available in the internet marketing arena: Search Engine marketing, blogging, YouTube, Social Media, etc. In simple language, the book explains how to use them.

4.   Corporate   Cyberwar

www.corporatecyberwar.com

Corporate Cyberwar chronicles the daily battle between technical criminals and law enforcement. As new and advanced ways to cheat and financially ruin companies are discovered, many authorities not only have to figure out ways to stop it, but they also have to create new laws in order to prosecute the perpetrators.

Tactic 5: Identify and Use the Right Productivity Tools

Additional Resources

1. Turnaround Handbook: Corporate Turnaround and Transformation

www.turnaroundhandbook.com

This is a comprehensive handbook on corporate transformation and turnaround. It provides other online resources that the reader can turn to for guidance. These include ebooks, Youtube videos, and poems on transforming the corporations.

2. Transformation Toolkit: Corporate Transformation to improve Productivity and Innovation

www.transformationtoolkit.com

The "Transformation Toolkit: Corporate Transformation to Improve Productivity and Innovation" provides the means to diagnose an ailing business organization, and then plan and pursue the steps to keep it alive and make it healthy.

3. Change Management Leadership

www.changemanagementleadership.com

The book teaches us how to handle the many crises that corporations may face. Bible characters such as Jesus, King David, Moses, Joshua, and the Apostle Paul are all great change managers.

4. Internet Turnaround: The use of internet marketing to turnaround companies

 www.turnaroundinternet.com

"Internet Turnaround" is a step by step guide that will enable you to discover the rules of winning in the internet business.

5. Link Baiting to improve your page ranking on search engines

www.linkbaitings.com

Link Baiting survives as the most productive marketing tool for Internet and SEO marketing. It has transformed this internet marketing tool into a fully established form of attracting visitors and increasing rankings.

6. Corporate Cyberwar

www.corporatecyberwar.com

Corporate Cyberwar chronicles the daily battle between technical criminals and law enforcement. As new and advanced ways to cheat and financially ruin companies are discovered, many authorities not only have to figure out ways to stop it, but they also have to create new laws in order to prosecute the perpetrators.

7. Ultimate Internet Marekting Strategies For Turbulent Times

www.ultimateinternetstrategy.com

Have you always wondered how numerous business owners across the globe have managed to market and advertise their brand and business so successfully online that internet visitors have felt compelled to consume their products and services?

Tactic 6: Innovate to Outsmart the Competition

Additional Resources

1.   Transformation Toolkit: Corporate Transformation to improve Productivity and Innovation

www.transformationtoolkit.com

The "Transformation Toolkit: Corporate Transformation to Improve Productivity and Innovation" provides the means to diagnose an ailing business organization, and then plan and pursue the steps to keep it alive and make it healthy.

2.   Change Management Leadership

www.changemanagementleadership.com

The failure to predict and address our current global financial problems can be directly attributed to poor leadership. It was bad and unprincipled leadership that brought us to the dismal situation we are in now. Fortunately, it will be good and principled leadership that can get us back on track.

Turnaround   Handbook: Corporate   Turnaround   and   Transformation
www.turnaroundhandbook.com

This is a very comprehensive handbook on corporate transformation and turnaround. It provides other online resources that the reader can turn to for guidance. These resources include ebooks, Youtube videos, and poems on transforming corporations.

Tactic 7: Take Action

Additional Resources

1. Post-Merger Integration: Improving shareholders' values after a merger
www.changemanagementorganizational.com
The majority of the merger and acquisitions destroy shareholders' values. This is because companies come together merely looking at the financial and strategic fits and fail to focus on integration fits such as cultural, operational, and other issues.

2. How to start a home spa business
www.homespabiz.com
For those looking to start a home business, this will be a useful book. It takes the reader with no knowledge on the spa business to understand why this is a lucrative business and how to immediately start one with no hassle.

3 . Fundamentals of Buying and Selling of Companies
www.restructuringspecialist.com
Written in a simple and easy-to-understood manner, this book tackles the complex topic of mergers and acquisitions and what to do look for when buying and selling companies.

4. Buying and selling of distressed company
www.restructuringexpert.com
Buying and selling of distressed company can be a very profitable venture. This is because you are buying at low price-earnings as the distressed company's shareholders are desperate to find

a white knight to save it. When the company is turned around, the valuation of the company can go up by many multiples of its original price.

5. Corporate Turnaround: Global Perspective

www.turnaroundguru.com

This presents a study of the various corporate turnaround techniques used all around the world eg China, Russia, Europe, Latin America etc.

6. Africa, The Next Economic Tiger: Lessons From Asia

Asia and Africa came out from colonialism in poverty. But Asia has raced ahead to become an economic miracle. Africa has been left behind. There are many lessons that Africa can learn from Asia

Appendix III – Online Resources For Corporate Turnaround

These online resources by Dr. Mike Teng cover the various phases of Corporate Turnaround.

Corporate Turnaround – Preliminary – Diagnosis

Corporate Turnaround: Nursing a sick company back to health

www.miketeng.com

Using medical analogies, *Corporate Turnaround: Nursing a Sick Company Back to Health* prescribes effective and easy-to-administer turnaround techniques in the right doses.

Business Diagnosis

www.restructuringcosts.com

This book provides a guide on how to determine the corporate health. It also provides a list of cost-cutting measures to help company manage its cash flow.

Inspirational Notebook

www.inspirationalnotebook.com

A book to inspire and encourage companies for corporate transformation and turnaround with poems, YouTube videos, and books outlines, *Inspirational Notebook is* also agood companion to have for one's note-taking .

Also visit Dr. Mike Teng's www.youtube.com/1103teng to watch the YouTube videos of some of the books.

Transformation Presentation 1

http://tinyurl.com/Transformationpresentation1

Most companies today need to go through corporate turnaround and transformation. Yet, many companies do not know how because they have not encountered such a protracted crisis like this one before. And many business schools do not teach the subject of corporate turnaround and transformation because many academic staff members do not have this experience. This protracted recession can mean significant challenges and problems for companies. Stay away from a desperate situation and save your company from the trouble of having to deal with a depression RIGHT NOW! The solution is to learn from the expert on how to manage the challenges. Avoid making the same mistakes that other people have made on restructuring. This talk not only shares how to restructure but also restructure into a competitive, innovative and flexible organization. This is part 1 of 3.

Transformation Presentation 2

http://tinyurl.com/Transformationpresentation2

This is part 2 of 3 in the series on corporate turnaround and transformation.

Transformation Presentation 3

http://tinyurl.com/Transformationpresentation3

This concludes the 3-part series on corporate turnaround and transformation.

Best-selling corporate turnaround books

http://tinyurl.com/turnaroundbooks

Corporate turnaround and transformation are essential in this global economic depression. Change management is the first step to be taken towards restoring and ensuring the health of companies that have been affected by this financial crisis. From a series of best-selling books by Dr. Michael Teng, you can learn everything there is to know about corporate turnaround, the buying and selling of companies, office politics, personal transformation, and successful competition in cyberspace.

Early diagnosis

http://tinyurl.com/earlydiagnosis

With this comprehensive toolkit you can determine the health of your organization as of a particular date. Use this handbook to identify possible symptoms of poor health early on. Probe into specific weak spots, prescribe solutions to fix problems, prioritize focus areas and treat with appropriate remedies.

Corporate Turnaround – Phase I – Surgery

Corporate Turnaround: Global perspective

www.turnaroundguru.com

A study of the various corporate turnaround techniques used all around the world, e.g., China, Russia, Europe, Latin America, etc.

Corporate Turnaround: Nursing a sick company back to health (Second Edition)

www.michaelteng.com

Following the success of the first edition which was a best-selling book in 2002, Dr Michael Teng revised the book to incorporate new strategies to handle new challenges facing the modern day corporations. Do not miss reading this book for the second time as it crystallizes some of the best-kept secrets in corporate turnaround and transformation.

You can also visit Dr. Mike Teng's www.youtube.com/1103teng to watch the YouTube videos of some of the books.

Corporate Turnaround to save company

http://tinyurl.com/corporateturnaround1

Sub-prime crisis, Bear Stearns, Freddie Mac, Fannie Mae, Lehman Brothers, AIG, Washington Mutual, Bradford & Bingley and Fortis. Governmental financial rescue, global recession: crisis after crisis. Will there be a Second Depression? What is next? For sure, all companies need to go through corporate turnaround to save them or transform them in the new landscape.

Corporate Transformation Centre - Corporate Hospital

http://tinyurl.com/corporatetransformationcentre

When you are sick, you visit a doctor for treatment. When you have cancer, you do not even visit the general practitioner, you visit an oncologist or cancer specialist. Yet, many sick companies do not seek help early enough. Similar to physical health, the key in a successful transformation is early diagnosis and treatment. Also, these sick companies do not know where to seek help for corporate turnaround. This is the rationale for setting up a corporate hospital or corporate transformation centre (CTC).

Corporate turnaround management for prosperity

http://tinyurl.com/corporateturnaround

There are many so-called corporate viruses that can affect the health of your company. The rapid changes of globalization and the slowdown that the global economy is now experiencing at a scary rate, are examples of corporate viruses. In addition to this, incompetent management is a serious cause of the lack of growth or the sickness of your company. Corporate Turnaround is the best solution. Recession is a part of the macroeconomic cycle. Therefore, it occurs after a certain period, but this time it is not the usual recession. The on-going recession is equivalent to the great Depression of the 1930s. This is the greatest virus that companies have encountered since World War II. Therefore, companies around the world have to take immediate measures to save themselves and do a corporate turnaround.

Corporate Turnaround – Phase II – Resuscitation

Fundamentals of Buying and Selling Companies

www.restructuringspecialist.com

This book is written in a simple and easy-to-understand manner and tackles the complex topic of mergers and acquisitions and what to do and look for when buying and selling companies.

Buying and Selling Distressed Companies

www.restructuringexpert.com

Investing in distressed assets can prove to be very profitable as they are at rock bottom prices. This book delves into the nitty-gritty of what to look for when identifying such gems.

Post-Merger Integration

www.changemanagementorganizational.com

Shareholders' values are often marginalised after a merger or acquisition. This is because companies that merge only look at the strategic and financial, but they fail to take care of the post-merger integration issues, such as cultural fit.

You can also visit Dr. Mike Teng's www.youtube.com/1103teng to watch the YouTube videos of some of his books.

Beware of the Merger

http://tinyurl.com/bewareofmerger

Merger is a good corporate turnaround and transformation strategy. However, the majority of mergers do not add value to the shareholders. This is because companies merge for all the wrong reasons: ego reasons with no homework done. CEOs find it quicker and more glamorous to grow by merging rather than grow organically. They do not integrate the stakeholders and organizations properly, thus it results in failure.

Post-Merger Integration

http://tinyurl.com/postmerger

Shareholders' values are often marginalised after a merger or acquisition. This video reminds us of companies that merge only looking at the pre-merger issues, e.g., strategic and financial, which are more exciting. They fail to take care of post-merger integration issues such as cultural fit.

Going for public listing

http://tinyurl.com/publiclisting

Many SMEs want to go for public listing so the founders can make their money and retire. However, these founders need to make sure their companies are ready. Corporate governance and compliance are getting tight and strict in many jurisdictions. There are advantages with public listing such as making the profile of the firm more visible. Outsiders feel more comfortable dealing with a listed company as its financial reporting is more transparent. Insiders also feel proud working for a listed firm.

Buying a company

http://tinyurl.com/buyingacompany

Everyone wants to be his or her own boss. The easiest way to do this is to have your own business. You can own a business and be your own boss. But to own a business, you either need to start your own business or buy an existing one. Starting a business is not for everyone but yes, just about anyone and everyone can buy an existing business.

Buying Distressed Companies

http://tinyurl.com/distressedassets

Distressed securities include stocks, bonds, or other financial claims of companies that are close to or have reached financial distress. If a company has filed for bankruptcy, it is under financial distress. This category also includes bank debt and non-performing loans. The company fails to make regular interest or principal payments, and trades at yields higher than those of similar dated treasuries. Once the financial distress becomes evident, there is panic selling and the company can then trade at deep discounts. At this stage, there presents an attractive opportunity to anyone who has analyzed the company's true worth. In recent years, firms such as hedge funds and private equity firms have been among the largest buyers of distressed securities. They hold the securities until they have appreciated.

Fundamentals of Buying and Selling of Companies

www.restructuringspecialist.com

This book is written in a simple and easy-to-understand manner and talks about the complex topic of mergers and acquisitions and what to do look and look for when buying and selling companies.

Corporate Turnaround – Phase III – Nursing

Turnaround Handbook: Corporate Turnaround and Transformation

www.turnaroundhandbook.com

This is a very comprehensive handbook on corporate transformation and turnaround. It provides other online resources that the reader can turn to for guidance and these include ebooks, Youtube videos, and poems on transforming the corporations. The handbook guides the reader on corporate transformation and turnaround at the strategic, tactical, and individual levels.

You can also visit Dr. Mike Teng's www.youtube.com/1103teng to watch related YouTube videos.

It is time to change the way we think (Re-think Singapore)

http://tinyurl.com/rethinksingapore

Singapore, like many other countries, is going through a period of changes both in business structure and the economy. The global economic recession has forced us to re-think the way that we used to earn a living. The rise of China and India has made it difficult for us to compete in pricing for quality products and services. Our traditional markets in the West are decimated and multi-national companies that we used to rely on for our domestic market are moving out. If we continue to rest on our past laurels, we will be doomed to failure. As matter of fact, our past successes are not workable anymore and we need to re-think, transform, and turnaround if we are to survive and prosper.

Turnaround, Transform Singapore

http://tinyurl.com/transformsingapore

The clarion call for the world economy and business environment is turnaround, transform, and change. What has made Singapore successful in the past will not see us through the next five years as the business landscape has changed dramatically.

Turbulent times call for inspiring leaders

http://tinyurl.com/leaderinturbulenttimes

The failure to predict and address our current global financial problems could be directly attributed to poor leadership. It was bad and unprincipled leadership that brought us to the dismal situation we are in now. Fortunately, it will be good and principled leadership that can get us back on track again.

END

www.ingramcontent.com/pod-product-compliance
Lightning Source LLC
Chambersburg PA
CBHW050102210326
41519CB00015BA/3798